Through Scotland with the Caledonian Railway

A.J. Mullay

'Wemyss Bay' Tank 955 at Cardonald.

Contents

Introduction	3
Building the Main Line	5
Mergers and Takeovers	23
Caledonian Railway Stations – I	27
Amalgamations	31
Locomotives to 1894	41
Water Schemes	50
Crossing the Solway	58
Underground and Overground	65
Callander & Oban	97
Locomotives 1894-1922	110
Racing Days	128
Caledonian Railway Stations – II	146
Accidents	149
Passenger Carriages	156
Steamers	162
Docks	166
Hotels	169
The End of the Caledonian Railway	172
Works Consulted	176

'If ever a great commercial enterprise became wrapped in an aura of romance, it was the Caledonian Railway …'
O.S. Nock.

Beattock Summit.

© 2010 Alexander Mullay
First Published in the United Kingdom, 2010
Stenlake Publishing Limited
54-58 Mill Square, Catrine, KA5 6RD
01290 551122
www.stenlake.co.uk

ISBN 9781840334913

Introduction

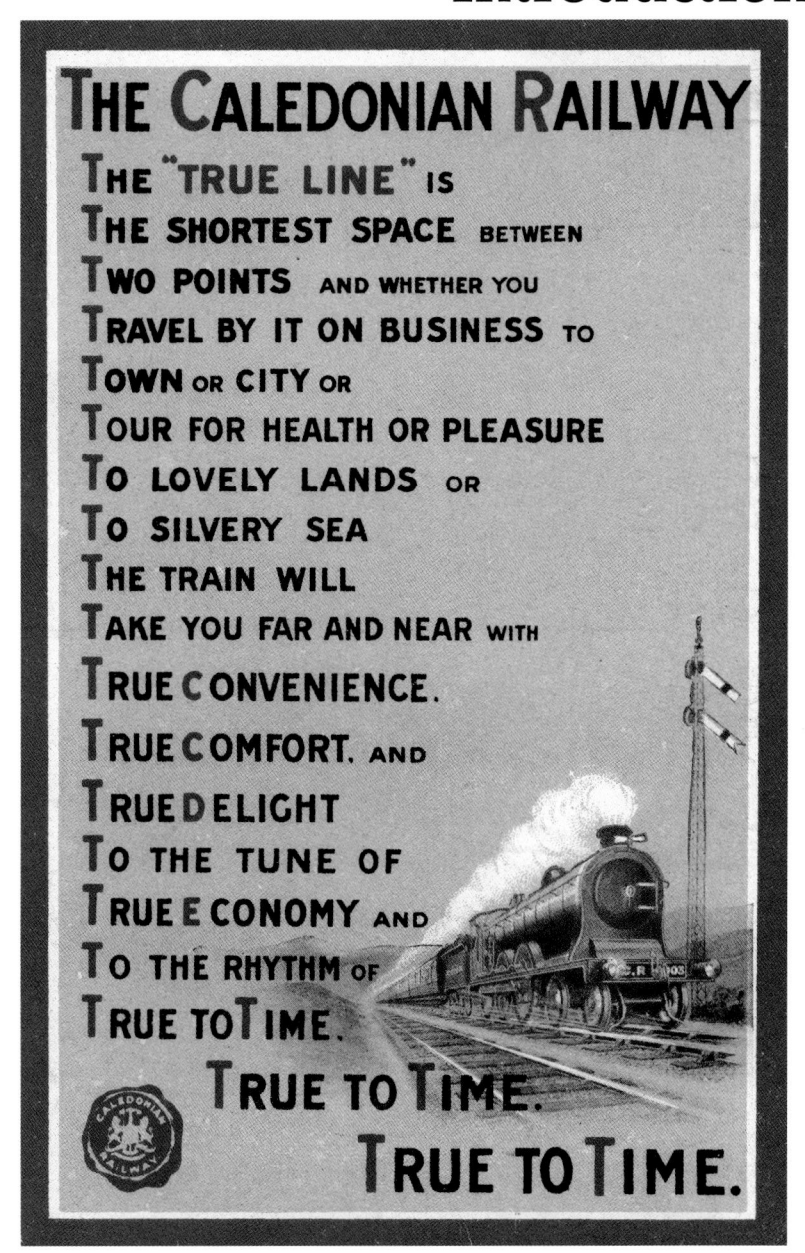

THE CALEDONIAN RAILWAY

THE "TRUE LINE" IS
THE SHORTEST SPACE BETWEEN
TWO POINTS AND WHETHER YOU
TRAVEL BY IT ON BUSINESS TO
TOWN OR CITY OR
TOUR FOR HEALTH OR PLEASURE
TO LOVELY LANDS OR
TO SILVERY SEA
THE TRAIN WILL
TAKE YOU FAR AND NEAR WITH
TRUE CONVENIENCE.
TRUE COMFORT. AND
TRUE DELIGHT
TO THE TUNE OF
TRUE ECONOMY AND
TO THE RHYTHM OF
TRUE TO TIME.
TRUE TO TIME.
TRUE TO TIME.

Although not Scotland's largest railway, the Caledonian Railway had a fair claim to being the greatest. Conceived as a main line connecting Edinburgh and Glasgow with England, it enjoyed government approval as the route to the south, even when it failed to be the first line to cross the Border through over-dependence on English investment.

Nevertheless, the 'Caley', with its graceful blue-liveried locomotives, its luxurious rolling-stock (including a Pullman observation car for its West Highland routes) and its extensive mineral traffic, was one of the most important transport enterprises in Europe – and one of the most stylish. Not for nothing did the Caledonian appropriate Scotland's coat of arms for its own. The Lord Lyon, King of Arms (Scotland's equivalent of the College of Heralds) appears not to have objected. In 1957, 34 years after the company had ceased to exist, railway historian O.S.Nock wrote 'The Caledonian never seemed to miss a single opportunity for adding touches of beauty, dignity, and elegance to its business of railroading'.

Despite its early difficulties, the company built a web of steel around Central Scotland, reaching to Aberdeen in the north, Oban in the west, and across the Solway to Cumberland in the south. Its services entered remote parts of Galloway and Argyllshire. It also built a major network of suburban lines in Glasgow, including an underground cross-city line, and an expensive line across north Edinburgh (which curiously remained unopened to passengers). Great stations for Glasgow and Edinburgh were built and additionally the company owned a share of those in Aberdeen, Perth and Carlisle, operated a major port at Grangemouth and furnished a fleet of steamers on the Clyde.

Ironically (in view of its name), with the implied emphasis on the *the* – the Caledonian Railway was floated with 77% of its funding from English shareholders. Historian C.J.A. Robertson went as far as to describe the Caledonian as 'an English railway in disguise'. All this proved to be a massive disadvantage as soon as even the feeblest of winds of recession began to blow in the 1840s and the company's masters found that calls made to its financial supporters fell on deaf ears. After all, the proponents of a West Coast main line had to see the Grand Junction finished and the Lakeland fells conquered before they could even start thinking about forging northwards from Carlisle across the rivers of the Debatable Land and addressing the foothills of the Lowthers.

By contrast, the Caledonian's greatest rival, the North British Railway (or NBR), was funded from Scottish fortunes. While dependent on an English partner company to complete an East Coast Main Line between the capital cities of England and Scotland, it was master of its own destiny in the short term, an Edinburgh company managed largely by Edinburgh men. They may have had more limited ideas than their Caledonian rivals, but they were able to build southwards quickly, and rapidly grew in confidence as the 'Railway Mania' flourished in the mid-1840s. Soon the Edinburgh company was effectively building a second main line to England (via Hawick) before the Caledonian could even be sure of building its first.

Nevertheless, there was no real comparison in the engineering standards between the Caledonian's route to Aberdeen (whether from Glasgow or from the West Coast Main Line at Law Junction) and the NBR's line from Edinburgh to Aberdeen. The latter was built in sections by different companies employing various contractors. The difference in quality was made painfully apparent (to the NBR) when the Caledonian regularly showed it a clean pair of heels in the 1895 Railway Race to the North.

If the North British Railway was, as C. Hamilton Ellis observed, 'a shabby tiger', the Caledonian was a gazelle!

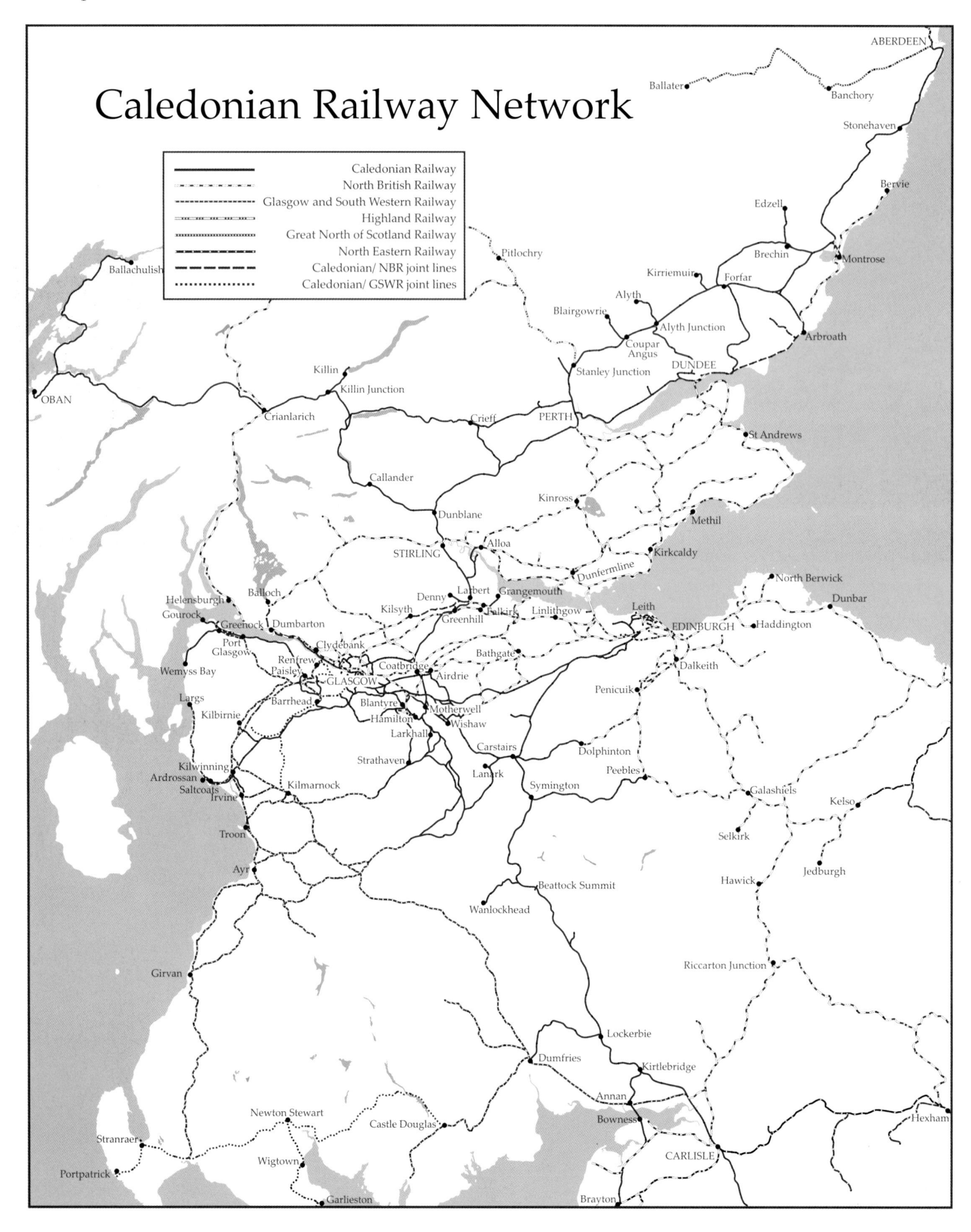

Caledonian Railway Network

———————	Caledonian Railway
—·—·—·—	North British Railway
− − − − −	Glasgow and South Western Railway
⊟⊟⊟⊟⊟	Highland Railway
⋮⋮⋮⋮⋮	Great North of Scotland Railway
━ ━ ━ ━	North Eastern Railway
– – – –	Caledonian/ NBR joint lines
··········	Caledonian/ GSWR joint lines

Carlisle.

Building the Main Line

One morning in the spring of 1846, an invading army marched into the Debatable Land between England and Scotland – and stopped. Instead of weapons, the thousands of 'soldiers' wielded tools. Instead of pillage and bloodshed, their intention was to break the earth. The Caledonian Railway was about to begin construction.

It might seem strange for a Scottish company – an overtly Scottish company – to begin building its main line in and from England, but there were two practical reasons for doing so. Firstly, it was hoped that men and horses could be transferred from the allied Lancaster and Carlisle Railway nearing completion to the south. Secondly, the urban approach into Glasgow had been secured by absorbing established railways, albeit mineral lines, and this comparatively easy method of building a major trunk route – one which the North British also used – will be examined in the next chapter.

Carlisle, Port Carlisle Junction.

Carlisle to Glasgow and Edinburgh.

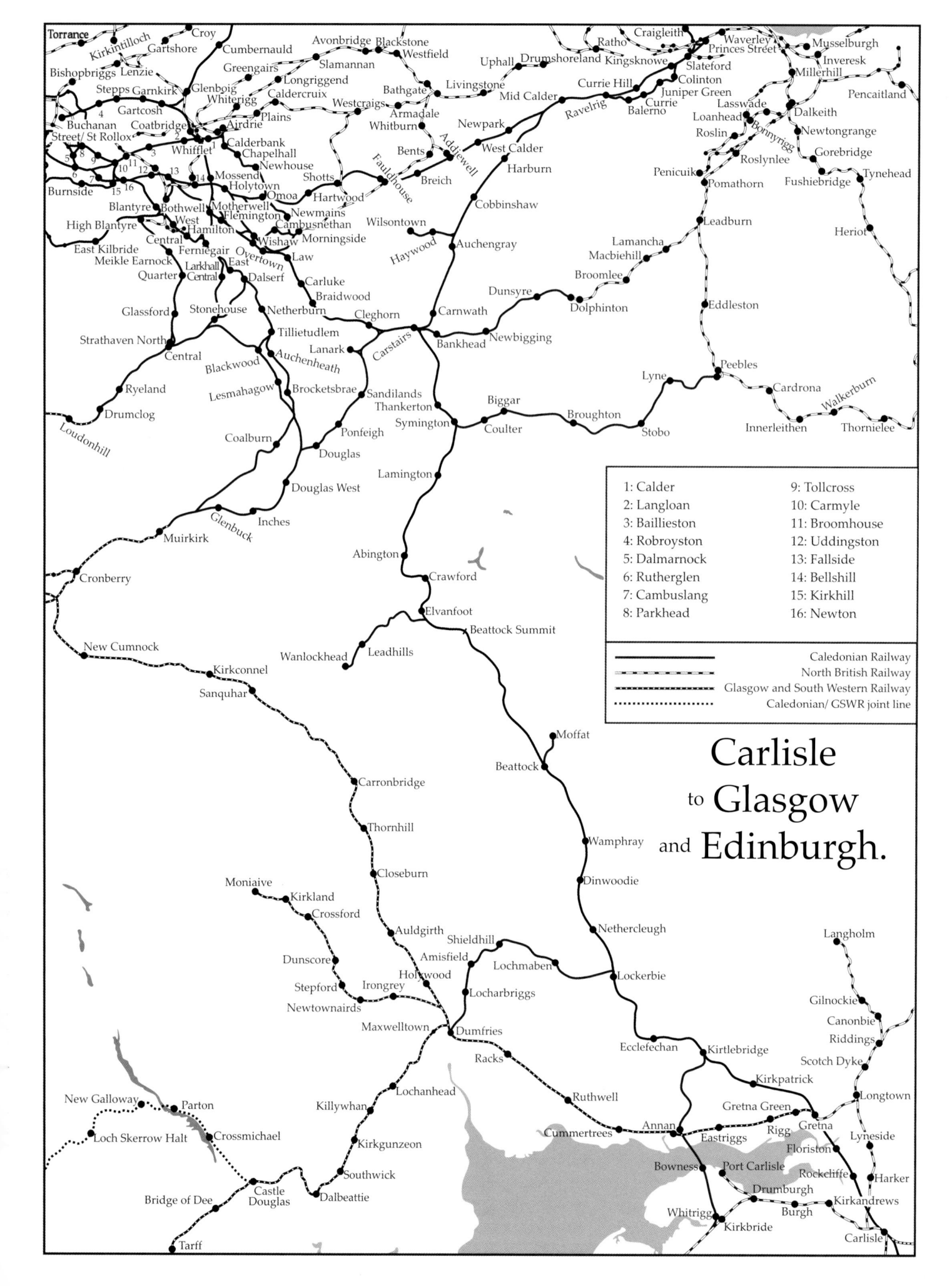

Key:
1: Calder
2: Langloan
3: Baillieston
4: Robroyston
5: Dalmarnock
6: Rutherglen
7: Cambuslang
8: Parkhead
9: Tollcross
10: Carmyle
11: Broomhouse
12: Uddingston
13: Fallside
14: Bellshill
15: Kirkhill
16: Newton

Lines:
- Caledonian Railway
- North British Railway
- Glasgow and South Western Railway
- Caledonian/ GSWR joint line

Gretna.

In the company's earliest years, the Caledonian's supporters had argued that it was the line between England and Scotland, officially approved by the government's Smith-Barlow Commission of 1841. This had been set up to investigate transport needs between London, Scotland, and Ireland, at a time when a government glorying in the concept of *laissez faire* rarely concerned itself with having a planned approach to any public matter. So important was this issue, however, that a national transport policy appeared necessary, and it was concluded that only one main line need connect England and Scotland, that being the one through Annandale and Carlisle.

Even the East Coast Main Line was to be rendered unnecessary, thanks to the Caledonian Railway's connection with the Lancaster & Carlisle and Grand Junction Railways, making the West Coast Main Line between the two countries a logical cross-Border route, splitting at what became Carstairs Junction, linking with both Edinburgh, the Scottish capital, and Glasgow, the main industrial centre.

Kirkpatrick.

All this was to be conditional on a start being made on construction within a reasonable time, and here the West Coast interest had a problem. So attractively logical did a line up the west of Great Britain appear, serving the interests (albeit not directly) of Birmingham, Liverpool, and Manchester, as well as London, Glasgow, and Edinburgh, that the company received much of its backing from English investors. That came close to being its undoing. With no less than three-quarters of its capital being promised by English speculators, it was inevitable that the southern part of the route, with its need to conquer the Lakeland Fells, would absorb what money was immediately available, leaving little for the extension on the Scottish side. In contrast, the eagerly (if poorly) constructed, North British section of the East Coast Main Line was largely Edinburgh-financed, and proceeded more quickly, just as a conditional finding of the Smith-Barlow Commission allowed it to do.

Ecclefechan.

Comparing the two prospectuses, the 'Caley's' printed in Westminster and the NBR's in Edinburgh, it's noticeable that the capital projection of the former was exactly twice that of the NBR, £1.8 million against £900,000. Share prices were £50 and £25 respectively. At this stage (March 1844) Lord Belhaven chaired the Provisional Committee, which was an impressive line-up of establishment names from both sides of the Border. In contrast, the NBR's prospectus (issued the previous year), showed no chairman's name, aristocratic or otherwise, but headed its committee list with the municipal heads of Edinburgh and Berwick – a down-to-earth statement of intent.

Dalveen Pass.

The Caledonian Railway finally received royal assent for its enabling Act on 31 July 1845, although it was not allowed to build some associated branch lines, including one to Dumfries through the Dalveen Pass (and what a line that would have been). The desire to tie in the county town of Dumfriesshire, the only sizeable town in the whole of the south-west of Scotland south of Ayr and Kilmarnock, was grounded on rapidly-acquired business realism on the part of the company's promoters.

The Caledonian's directors were becoming only too aware of the dearth of population served by their line through the central Borderland. The company's more detailed plans in 1846 showed that there would be only one 'First Class' station – Lockerbie – in the 30 miles between Gretna and Beattock and that was for a burgh of less than 4,000 people.

St Rollox to Carlisle goods train at Beattock Summit. The train includes the 'dead' LNWR 1344 *en route* **to Crewe.**

Lockerbie.

LOCKERBIE C.R.
4-4-0 - No. 901.

In contrast, the Glasgow & South Western Railway line intended to link Glasgow and Carlisle would bisect the busy Ayrshire coalfield (and the lesser one at Sanquhar in Dumfriesshire) as well as the bustling towns of Kilmarnock and Dumfries. This line also commanded the rail approaches to the south-west peninsula where the North Channel ports of Portpatrick and Stranraer are situated.

In retrospect, one wonders if the Caledonian supporters in the late 1840s wished that they could have utilised the Ayrshire-Nithsdale route of the GSWR and ditched the concept of a Crewe-like junction at Carstairs, especially since Edinburgh was now forging its own route to England down the east coast. That there is some evidence that they seriously considered re-routing around 1847 is shown by the actions of Annandale landowner John James Hope-Johnstone in campaigning successfully to keep the Caledonian, of which he happened to be chairman at the time, focused on its plans for a railway north through Lockerbie, by organising a public meeting to motivate public opinion. Ironically, he chose Dumfries in which to do this!

Wamphray.

Beattock.

Moffat.

Moffat.

Railway builders optimistically believed that the 'iron road' would stimulate business wherever it went, explaining some of the extraordinarily unremunerative railways (some built and some just projected) throughout the UK. Nevertheless, a company with such fragile resources as the Caledonian could hardly be blamed for hedging its bets by trying to tie Dumfries into its network, while cheerfully doing what it could to strangle rival concerns which already embraced the town.

By the early 1850s all this rivalry had been resolved, although hardly amicably, with the Caledonian at one time being legally permitted to work all the projected GSWR's traffic between Gretna and Carlisle, effectively blocking the rival line. This advantage proved unsustainable, possibly because sympathetic parliamentarians, including the Caledonian's own supporter the Duke of Buccleuch, were horrified at such a restraint of trade, which might lead in turn to the GSWR seeking a unified approach to the Border City with either the Newcastle and Carlisle Railway, or the North British Railway, which hoped to extend its Hawick Branch southwards. Suffice to say, that by the mid-1850s, the Caledonian permitted the smaller company running-powers over the nine-mile Gretna-Carlisle stretch.

Elvanfoot.

King's visit to Abington. The Station.

Symington.

Thankerton.

Carstairs.

Carluke.

The 'Caley' had by this time realised that branch lines could drain a railway company of its hard-won capital and ceased to agitate for its loop line through (or any line at all into) Dumfries, as well as abandoning its plans to reach Langholm and Brampton. The Caledonian eventually built into Dumfries in the mid-1860s by a branch line from Lockerbie, largely because it could argue it required access to its detached section, the joint Portpatrick line running westwards through Galloway.

Whifflet.

Coatbridge

As the spring of 1846 broadened into summer, the new 'army' in the Debatable Land grew and consolidated and by August 1847 20,000 men were at work, aided by four contractors' locomotives and 3,500 horses. The horses may have been well-behaved but the human workers were not! Known as 'navvies' (from 'navigators', the men who had cut the canals to create a major transport network all over Britain during the previous 70 years), these were mainly Irishmen seeking employment prospects better than they could find in their native island (although Thomas Carlyle, born at Ecclefechan in the Annan valley, maintained that workers from the north of England were the worst behaved). By October 1846 the Dumfriesshire police were asking for a permanent 'lockup house' to be built at the company's expense near the Border and the cavalry had already been called out to suppress a workers' riot at Lockerbie.

It appears that the management was not of a much higher standard. The new company had already made a symbolic clearing of ground at Beattock Summit, perhaps to satisfy investors that some action was actually underway, but there was an unforeseen consequence. Within a few months, the Caledonian's managers were faced with a bill for customs duties on the import of 'mud wagons, barrows, and planks" from England!

Beattock presented a major problem for the new line. At one time, the Beattock Pass through the Lowther Hills (connecting the valley of the Evan Water, flowing south to the Annan, and the upper Clyde, flowing northwards) was considered too steep for a railway venture. On his first survey, Joseph Locke is believed to have turned for home as soon as he arrived at Beattock, and he required some persuasion not to plump for the rival route through Nithsdale. Not only did the gradient appear too steep for trains ascending – around 1 in 80 for ten miles – but he believed that the brake power then available would be insufficient to guarantee a safe descent. Fortunately for Hope-Johnstone and his colleagues in the 'Annandale' lobby, railway technology developed so quickly in the 1840s as to allay Locke's fears. Interestingly, Joseph Locke later settled at Moffat for his well-earned retirement amid the landscape he had found so forbidding as an engineer.

Garnkirk

Stepps.

Beattock Bank never ceased to be an operational problem for the Caledonian Railway and its successors, for as long as steam engines were the principal element of motive power. The village situated at the foot of the bank still includes former workers' cottages, and there was a locomotive depot here for 120 years to supply additional power for the 'banking' of trains (i.e. attaching an additional engine at the rear of the train). The Bank was the major engineering work on the new line, although there were also important viaducts over the Eden at Etterby, the Esk near Mossband and the Annan near Wamphray. North of Beattock Summit, a number of smaller viaducts straddle the burgeoning Clyde, but it was the necessity to bridge the Clyde within Glasgow that was to be more of a practical problem for the company.

Buchanan Street Station.

The line was opened between Carlisle and Beattock on 9 September 1847, and between the border city and Glasgow and Edinburgh on 15 February 1848. To reach Edinburgh from Carstairs, the line had to be taken over Cobbinshaw Summit, yet another hill for a London-Edinburgh train to climb when travelling on the West Coast Route. Sensibly, the Caledonian allowed Edinburgh's water authorities to lay a pipeline beside the railway eastwards from Cobbinshaw Reservoir, to which the company had free access for its operational needs.

Carstairs.

For the Caledonian directors, the line's opening could not be accomplished quickly enough, and a passenger train was arranged between Carlisle and Beattock, carrying local dignitaries and representatives of the allied Lancaster & Carlisle Railway. On 9 September 1847, a day of constant rain, the VIPs were taken to Beattock, forty miles along the virgin railway, in two hours. A 'cold collation' was served at Beattock, with the usual self-congratulatory speeches being delivered. The party returned to Carlisle without mishap (in contrast the NBR had suffered a fatality on board its first return train, 15 months earlier) and a limited service began shortly afterwards.

Carnwath.

Right from the start of operations, the Caledonian adopted what it called 'London time' for its Carlisle-Beattock service, when travellers arriving in Carlisle from the south had to adjust their watches, discovering that they were in a different time-zone, with the border city 12 minutes behind London!

The first Caledonian train out of Glasgow left Townhead the 15 February following (1848). This was a 'press trip', and the Glasgow Herald's description of the First Class accommodation is quoted in the later chapter on passenger rolling stock. At 9.45 that morning the new train began its journey along the Garnkirk and Wishaw & Coltness lines to Overtown, before joining a main line worthy of the name. In the Clyde Valley, the journalists were amused to greet both up and down mail coaches, the guard of one of them stoutly refusing to return the waves and cheers of the railway passengers.

Wilsontown.

Cobbinshaw.

Mid Calder, staff.

At Beattock, the travellers were greeted by Caledonian chairman James Hope-Johnstone and engineer Joseph Locke. The train had experienced no trouble in descending the famous bank, whose gradient Locke had initially believed would be too steep for any brake system to deal with. Not much time was spent at Beattock – it being February after all – and the return up the bank went sufficiently well not to merit a mention in the newspaper reports. At Float (later renamed Carstairs), the Edinburgh portion was detached, taking the Caledonian directors with it, to face a vital meeting in the capital.

With the line only starting its commercial operations throughout its length, the railway's contractors presented the Caledonian promoters with a bill for a quarter of a million pounds. Badly behind schedule, with virtually no income to speak of, with no termini built in either Glasgow or Edinburgh, the Caledonian was on the point of foundering before it had really begun. Fortunately, railway directors were becoming more adept at dealing with the financial demands of their contractors and were considerably assisted by the suggestion from Joseph Locke that the construction costs rendered were excessive and that anyway, if the sum was written off, the contractors could salvage much of the material they had assembled in the construction! It was dangerously close to being a breach of contract by the Caledonian, but the directors cunningly went on to offer another contract altogether, for maintenance over the next seven years, in the knowledge or hope that over the period revenue would be available to enable the company to pay these bills. Architect William Tite made himself unpopular by arguing that some station costs had been overlooked. His commission for an Edinburgh terminus unsurprisingly vanished without trace and his colleague, William Burn, was frozen out of a later design competition. Nevertheless, for the moment, the 'Caley' directors were 'off the hook'.

Mid Calder Station

Mid Calder.

Kingsknowe.

Princes Street Station.

One of the recurring aspects which face the historian looking into transport matters before 1846, is the aggression of the Caledonian company and its supporters. Not yet troubled by the detailed niceties of construction, or of trying to organise Napoleonic-style workforces assembled by the contractors, the 'Caley's officials were free to harass other companies, who were already wrestling with practical constructional problems, by avariciously announcing extensions and branches to any town they could find on a Scottish map! A good example was Peebles, which in February 1846 was the ridiculous object of a treaty between the NBR and the CR. The latter company graciously consented not to build lines east of Peebles, if the NBR agreed not to construct a (hastily-planned and announced) line from Peebles to Biggar. Yet the NBR was not yet within 20 miles of Peebles (indeed, that town's first railway was staunchly independent of the NBR to begin with), while the Caledonian had never turned a wheel anywhere. No wonder this period is known as the 'Railway Mania'

The Caledonian also realised that its enabling legislation gave it an almost manorial right to the area around Gretna Green, not only choking off (to begin with) the Glasgow & South Western Railway approach from Glasgow through Dumfries, but also effectively preventing the North British Railway from coming down through the Mosspaul Pass from Hawick. In that particular blocking move, the Caledonian was to be completely successful, condemning the NBR to construct a more roundabout route through the wilds of Liddesdale.

In 1848, the Caledonian even considered a takeover of the Newcastle & Carlisle Railway, an established line which the Scottish company was in no financial state to bid for. Not surprisingly, the Newcastle & Carlisle directors, who may have been using the Caledonian as a bidder to force up the price of their line, rejected the 'Caley' offer as 'inadequate'.

Princes Street Station.

Between Glasgow & Edinburgh

West Calder

21

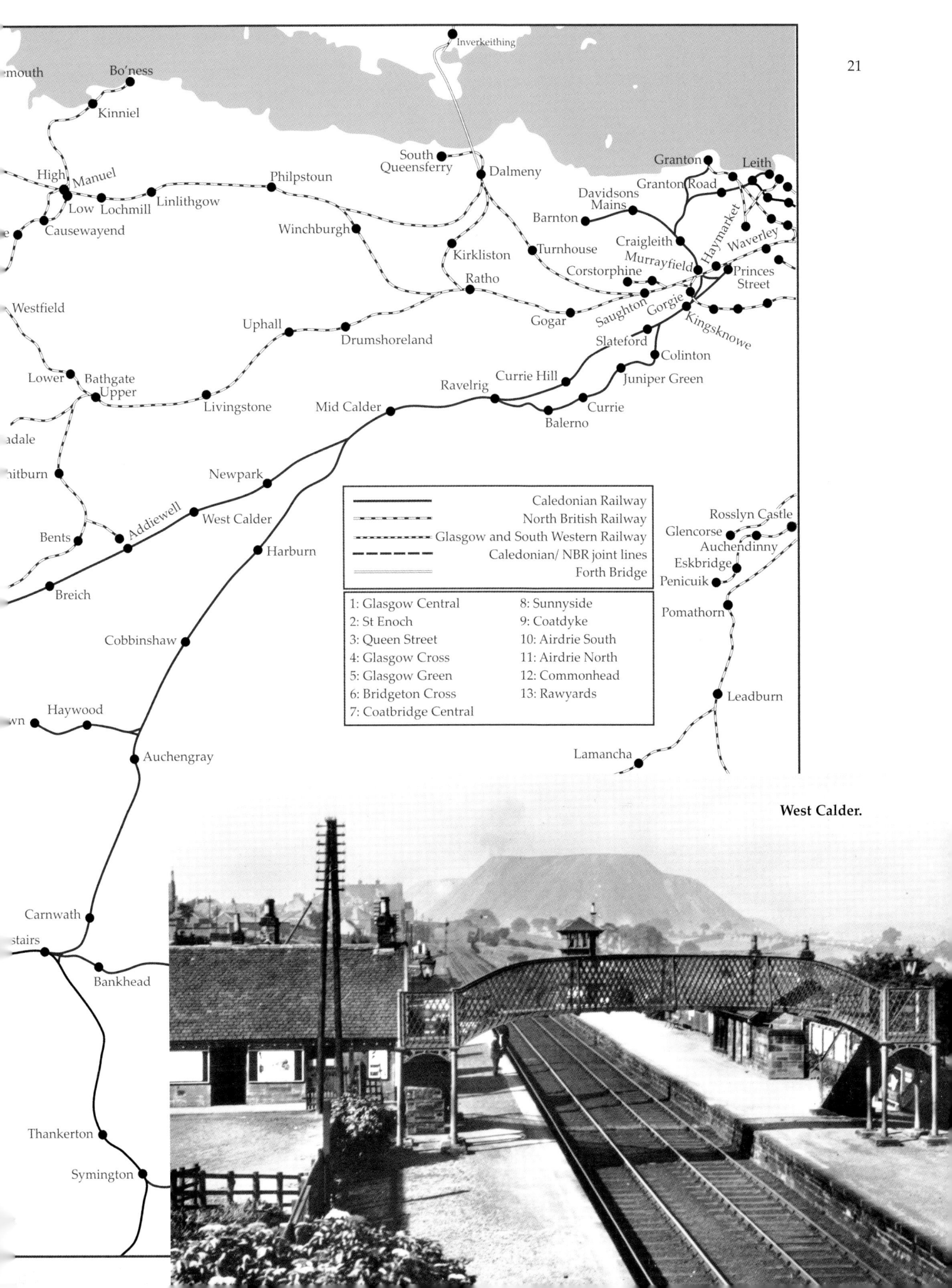

	Caledonian Railway
	North British Railway
	Glasgow and South Western Railway
	Caledonian/ NBR joint lines
	Forth Bridge

1: Glasgow Central
2: St Enoch
3: Queen Street
4: Glasgow Cross
5: Glasgow Green
6: Bridgeton Cross
7: Coatbridge Central
8: Sunnyside
9: Coatdyke
10: Airdrie South
11: Airdrie North
12: Commonhead
13: Rawyards

West Calder.

Addiewell.

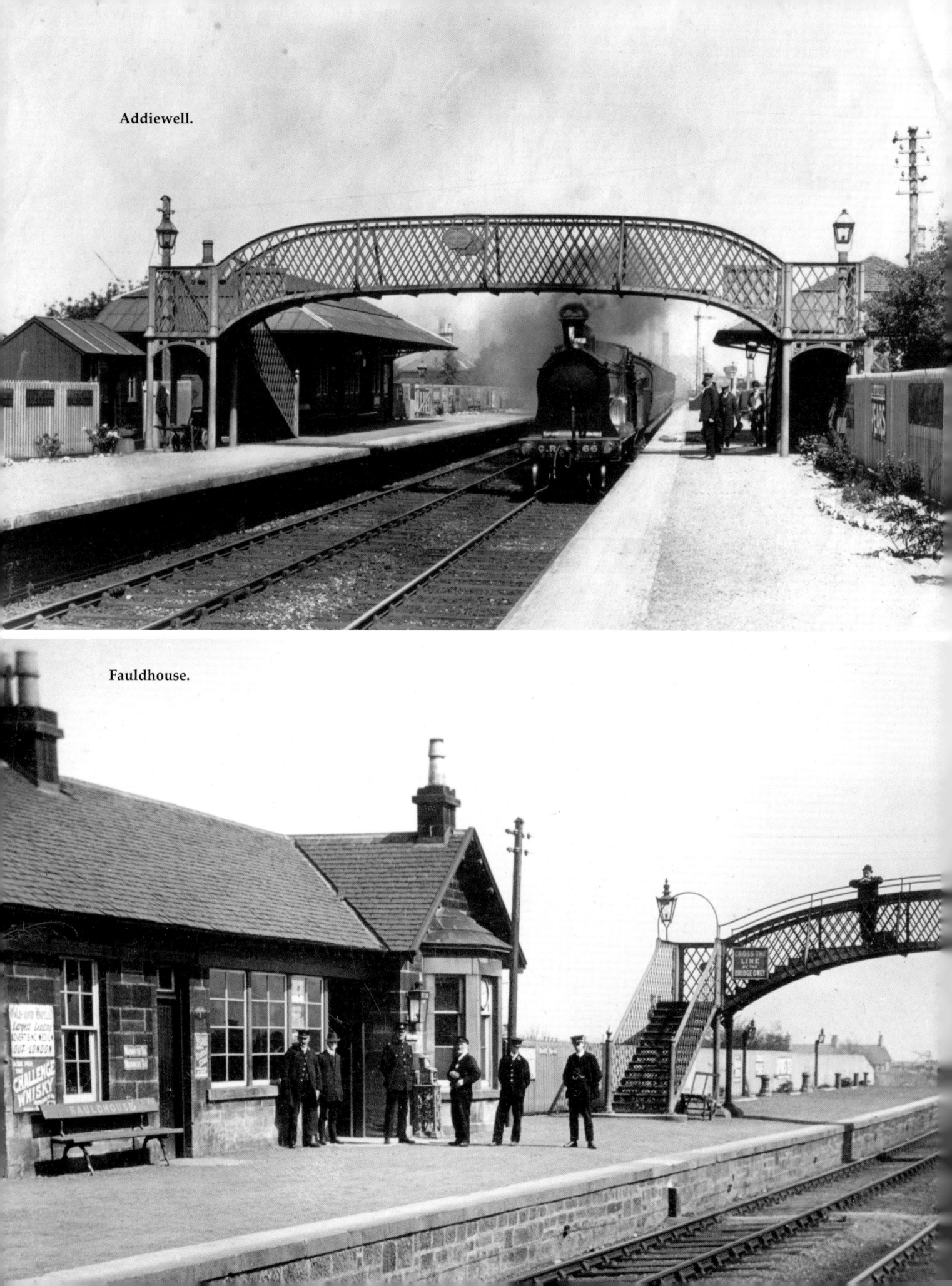

Fauldhouse.

Mergers and Takeovers

Shotts.

BATON EXCURSION LEAVING SHOTTS STATION.

Central Scotland had a considerable network of mineral railways operating by the 1840s – the first had been licensed by the old Scottish Parliament as early as 1606 – and Glasgow had a number of these working on either side of the Clyde once the Industrial Revolution was underway.

Prominent among these was the Garnkirk and Glasgow (with Coatbridge added to the name from 1844). This was a 'Scotch gauge' line (54 inches) running from the Wishaw and Coltness line at Whifflet (north of Motherwell and on the south side of modern day Coatbridge) into the north of Glasgow, near Port Dundas. The Wishaw and Coltness brought Lanarkshire coal towards the city and the location of these two unassuming lines gave the proposed Caledonian Railway a means of accessing Glasgow without too much expense. Both of these smaller companies therefore had to be acquired and then re-gauged, with the Caledonian planning to build southwards from Garriongill.

Shotts.

This was a comparatively cheap means of entering the Glasgow conurbation and enabled the company to avoid having to entertain property claims at a time when many landowners were beginning to perceive railways as a 'golden goose', but initially it involved the payment of tolls and presented the Caledonian with a series of Glasgow termini which were neither geared to passenger traffic nor important intercity traffic.

The reality of using existing railways to reach Glasgow was brought home early in March 1850 to CR stockholders, many of whom had probably never visited the line, when consulting engineer John Collister pointed out that express trains were now having to cross a single line wooden viaduct on the Wishaw and Coltness – "This is very objectionable to be upon a portion of a passenger main line", he opined, in case the speculators had failed to grasp that for themselves.

Omoa.

The wooden Jerviston Viaduct on the Wishaw and Coltness Railway. In 1857 it was superseded by a new viaduct about a mile away, in 1922 it was demolished and the stone from the piers reused in the Gleneagles Hotel.

Bellshill.

Chapelhall.

Newmains.

Baillieston.

Staff at Airdrie.

Staff at Bothwell.

Caledonian Railway Stations – part 1

The first Caledonian trains operating in and out of Glasgow made use of what was a glorified coal depot at Townhead, built by the Garnkirk & Glasgow Company on the north side of the Clyde, not far from St. Rollox. Not the least of its drawbacks was that both passengers and freight were liable for road tolls when walking or being transported to and from the city via the Inchbelly Road. This arrangement had been simplified nine years before the Caledonian arrived at the station, but a lump sum still had to be paid annually to the road trust by the Garnkirk company. So the 'Caley' was probably relieved to be able to take occupation of its own Glasgow station, also on the north bank of the Clyde.

Glasgow's Buchanan Street Station opened to passengers on 1 November 1849, and to goods on New Year's Day 1850, but was "subject to the casualties of weather", according to CR Board Minutes, because of the lack of overhead cover. Facilities improved, with the Board hurriedly authorising £1,500 to be spent on a water tank, sheds, and forges. Over the decades, Buchanan Street handled the principal Caledonian Railway traffic, with the exception of suburban trains, the terminus becoming something of a backwater following the opening of Central Station in 1879. After this, London and Edinburgh services were lost to the new terminus, but trains to Dundee, Perth, and Oban still used Buchanan Street. There were five platforms, only two of which exceeded 650 feet in length. Their width was not great either, a Fair reveller falling from one of them under the wheels of a train in 1902, an accident from which the Caledonian was lucky to escape liability in court. The platform awnings always had a temporary air, until the LMS replaced them with steel-framed glazed awnings (and these only 'second-hand', from Ardrossan North!). This took place in 1932, when a new concourse façade, consisting of steel frame covered with wood cladding, was built.

Buchanan Street Station.

Carstairs Junction. Apl. 25. 1913.

Demolishing Carstairs Junction. Apl. 27. 1913.

In their history of Glasgow stations, Johnston and Hume opine 'in this form, the station had something of the charm of a country terminus', they also quote the late Professor Jack Simmons as describing Buchanan Street Station as 'easily the most abominable in Western Europe'. It is abominable no more, having closed in 1966, when most of its services were transferred to Queen Street Station.

Of those stations planned between Carlisle and Carstairs back in 1846, only four were to be built to 'First Class' specifications – Springfield (Gretna), Lockerbie, Beattock and Abington. Within two years, Gretna residents had to point out to the 'Caley' that the construction of 'their' station in England, immediately south of the River Sark, ensured that passengers were forced to undergo Customs searches (for hidden alcohol, whose excise rates differed on each side of the Border) when walking between Gretna and Gretna Station! The company did nothing in response, but fortunately cross-Border Customs rates were soon abolished.

Lockerbie was the biggest town on the line, although with a population of less than 4,000 before the middle of the century. There no fewer than 12 'Second Class' stations, including Carstairs itself. Despite being included in this lower grade of stopping-place, Carstairs Junction boasted an overall roof (costing £200) spanning two narrow platforms and three tracks, although no refreshment facilities were authorised. The layout here was to remain substantially the same until 1913.

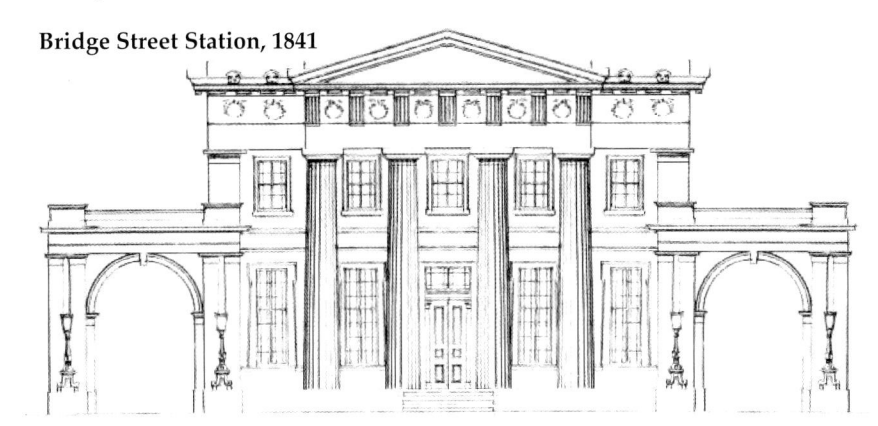

Bridge Street Station, 1841

With services between Glasgow and the Renfrewshire coast to cater for after the amalgamations of the 1850s, the Caledonian soon became a partial proprietor of a second terminus in Glasgow, at Bridge Street. This had opened on the south side of the Clyde in 1841, with the river flowing not far away behind the buffer-stops. With four platforms and eight tracks, this terminus was fronted by an impressive four-column Doric portico (although an alternative, more 'appropriate', entrance was hastily found for Third Class passengers!).

The Caledonian found itself sharing this station with the GSWR, which was well established here. Enmity between the two companies was not slow to develop – despite the sharing of Paisley traffic – and matters came to a head when the station was physically divided by a wall and railings from the mid-1870s, forcing passengers changing trains to make a circular journey of 400 yards out of the station and back again to a neighbouring platform. Bridge Street Station had a complicated history, well told by Johnston and Hume in their book on Glasgow stations. Suffice to say that the GSWR were to leave Bridge Street to their 'Caley' rivals, who found that they had no use for it after 1904. The roof was dismantled in the following year, and the portico demolished in 1971.

CR Railway station proposed for Glasgow, 1848.

Proposed Lothian Road Station, 1848.

To call Edinburgh's Caledonian terminus 'Princes Street' was inaccurate, the station opening first in Lothian Road, and later in Rutland Street. The Lothian Road site was supposed to be temporary, with renowned architect William Tite commissioned to build a station worthy of the Scottish capital – home, it should be remembered, to the Caledonian Railway Company offices in its early years. However, fiscal restraints prevailed, and the city had to tolerate a wooden four-platform structure facing the road approximately where the Sheraton Hotel is now. In fact, a recent biographical dictionary of architects credits Tite with having built a station here in 1847. The edifice, which was cobbled together here, lasted to 1870 when an enlarged terminus was constructed closer to Princes Street, the original site becoming part of Lothian Road Goods Yard. The 'new' terminus lasted only 20 years, with fire in what one writer called 'this wooden shanty' making rebuilding mandatory.

Princes Street Station.

Amalgamations

Interestingly, the army beginning the construction of the West Coast Main Line in the Debatable Land just north of Carlisle was starting the actual Caledonian line. The company name was synonymous with the concept of a 'national' main line up the centre of the country.

The Glasgow section of this would be, to begin with, rather less than a trunk route, but the grand concept was certainly being continued to destinations north of Glasgow and Edinburgh.

The independent companies making possible this foray northwards to Aberdeen were:

Scottish Central Railway	Castlecary to Perth
Scottish Midland Railway	Perth to Coupar Angus
Newtyle & Coupar Angus Railway	Coupar Angus to Newtyle (Alyth)
Newtyle & Glamis Railway	Newtyle to Glamis
Scottish Midland Junction Railway	Glamis to Forfar
Arbroath & Forfar Railway	Forfar to Guthrie
Aberdeen Railway	Guthrie to Aberdeen

These disparate companies were part of the vision of a grand trunk line running northwards up the spine of Britain. The biggest of these northern companies was the Scottish Central Railway. Conceived locally in 1844 as a means of connecting Perth with the Forth and Clyde valleys, this company rapidly fell into the Caledonian's plan (almost certainly the plan formulated and championed by Hope-Johnstone) for a national trunk route from London to the far north. Despite this, the company had a character and spirit of its own, and a very partisan spirit it was. Its first Secretary was the Town Clerk of Perth, and local surveyors gave their services freely to the company – not something that happened very often in the madcap Railway Mania!

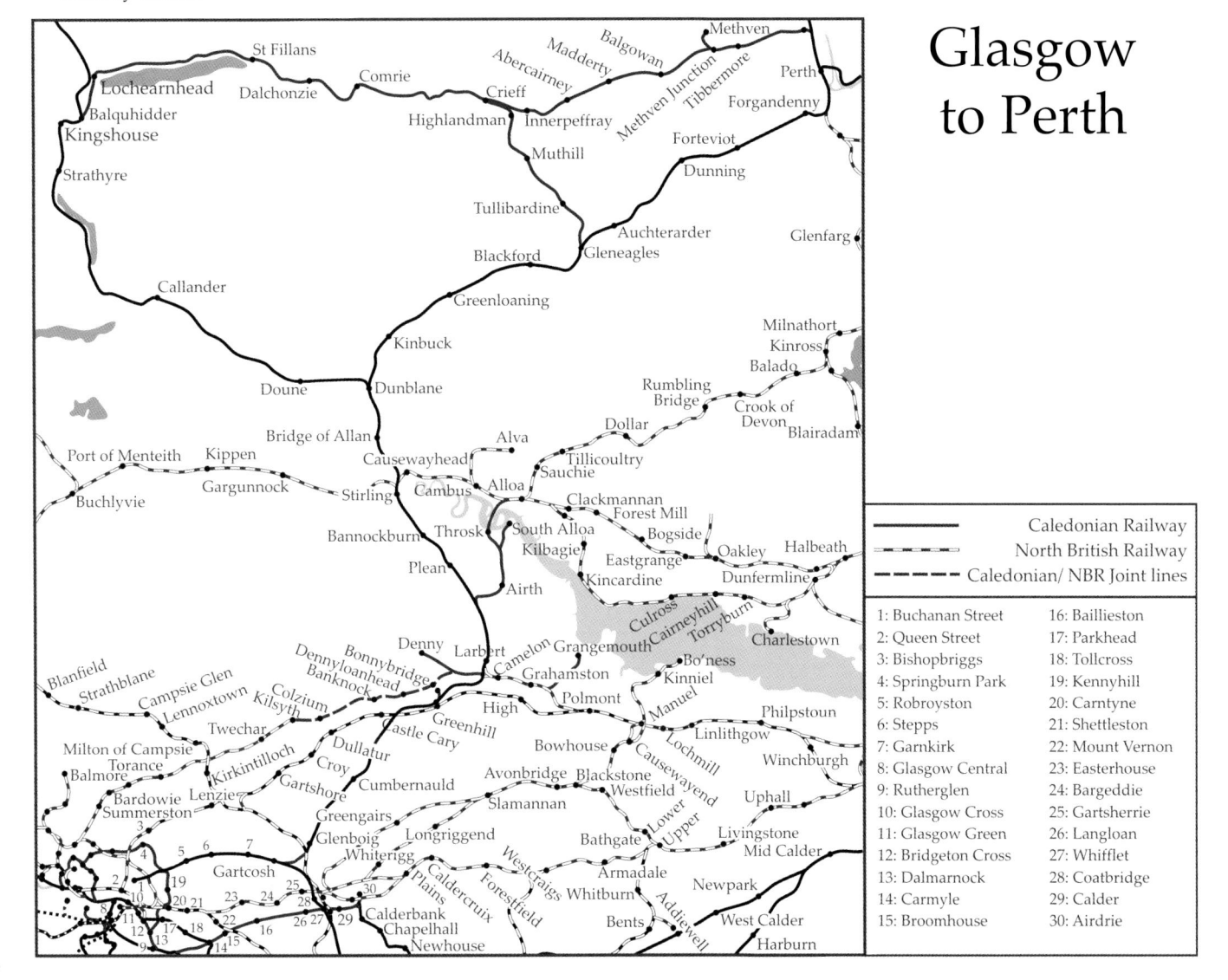

Glasgow to Perth

Legend:
— Caledonian Railway
—•— North British Railway
— — Caledonian/ NBR Joint lines

1: Buchanan Street
2: Queen Street
3: Bishopbriggs
4: Springburn Park
5: Robroyston
6: Stepps
7: Garnkirk
8: Glasgow Central
9: Rutherglen
10: Glasgow Cross
11: Glasgow Green
12: Bridgeton Cross
13: Dalmarnock
14: Carmyle
15: Broomhouse
16: Baillieston
17: Parkhead
18: Tollcross
19: Kennyhill
20: Carntyne
21: Shettleston
22: Mount Vernon
23: Easterhouse
24: Bargeddie
25: Gartsherrie
26: Langloan
27: Whifflet
28: Coatbridge
29: Calder
30: Airdrie

Garnqueen.

An early approach from the Caledonian – before that company had turned a wheel – to take over the nascent Scottish Central Railway was politely rebuffed, but links with the bigger concern were forged by the SCR's appointment of Englishmen Joseph Locke and John Errington as engineers. They were building the Caledonian's main line and had quite enough on their plate in designing a line to conquer Beattock. The appointment of Scotland's own John Miller, engineer of the Edinburgh & Glasgow Railway, which the SCR would certainly connect with in the Greenhill area, might have seemed more logical, as the company's historian, Peter Marshall, points out.

Another appointment which caused surprise at the time was that of Alexander Allan as Locomotive Superintendent of the SCR a few years later, in 1853. Allan was probably the most influential engineer of the decade, the louvred splashers of his engines giving his designs an unforgettable appearance. At the time of his appointment at Perth, Allan was second-in-command at Crewe Works, and he was popularly regarded as the strength behind the throne of Francis Trevithick. Indeed, some modern reference works list Allan equally with the nominal loco superintendents of the LNWR, Trevithick and McConnell. For him to move to Perth was an interesting comment on how important Allan saw the Scottish Central Railway to be, and although he failed to land the Caledonian post of Locomotive Superintendent, which became available in 1856, that may have been because at the time he was advising the Highland Railway on its motive power also!

Glenboig.

Glenboig.

The Scottish Central Railway would not be absorbed by its southern neighbour until 1865, by which time it had itself taken over the Callander & Oban company which was to give the Caledonian its most romantic, but also most troublesome, line.

All the Caledonian had to do to connect up with these northern railways (or would-be railways, for not all were built in the late 1840s, nor would they long remain as independent companies) was to connect to Castlecary (actually Greenhill, not far from Falkirk). Acquiring rights over the Wishaw and Coltness line brought the Caledonian to Gartsherrie, near Coatbridge. From here the 'Caley' built a spur to Cartgill on the Monkland and Kirkintilloch Railway (renamed the Monkland Railway from 1848), believing that this would soon be acquired, like the other mineral lines in the area. Consequently, running-powers were leased from the Monkland company to take Caledonian trains northwards back on to their own metals at Garnqueen, and then on through Glenboig and points north, while trains from Glasgow would come down from Gartcosh and would never leave CR tracks.

Cumbernauld.

Greenhill.

But a problem was to emerge here. A cuckoo's egg had been laid! The 52 chains (nearly three-quarters of a mile) of the Monkland line had been made available for Caledonian running (for a down payment of £750, and then a toll system), but the company's directors could never have imagined that this would one day make them dependent on the goodwill of the North British Railway, then far away in its eastern fastness! For the Monkland company was taken over, not by the Caledonian, but by the Edinburgh & Glasgow Railway. This was one merger that the Caledonian failed to make – and they paid dearly for it.

Larbert Station.

Stirling.

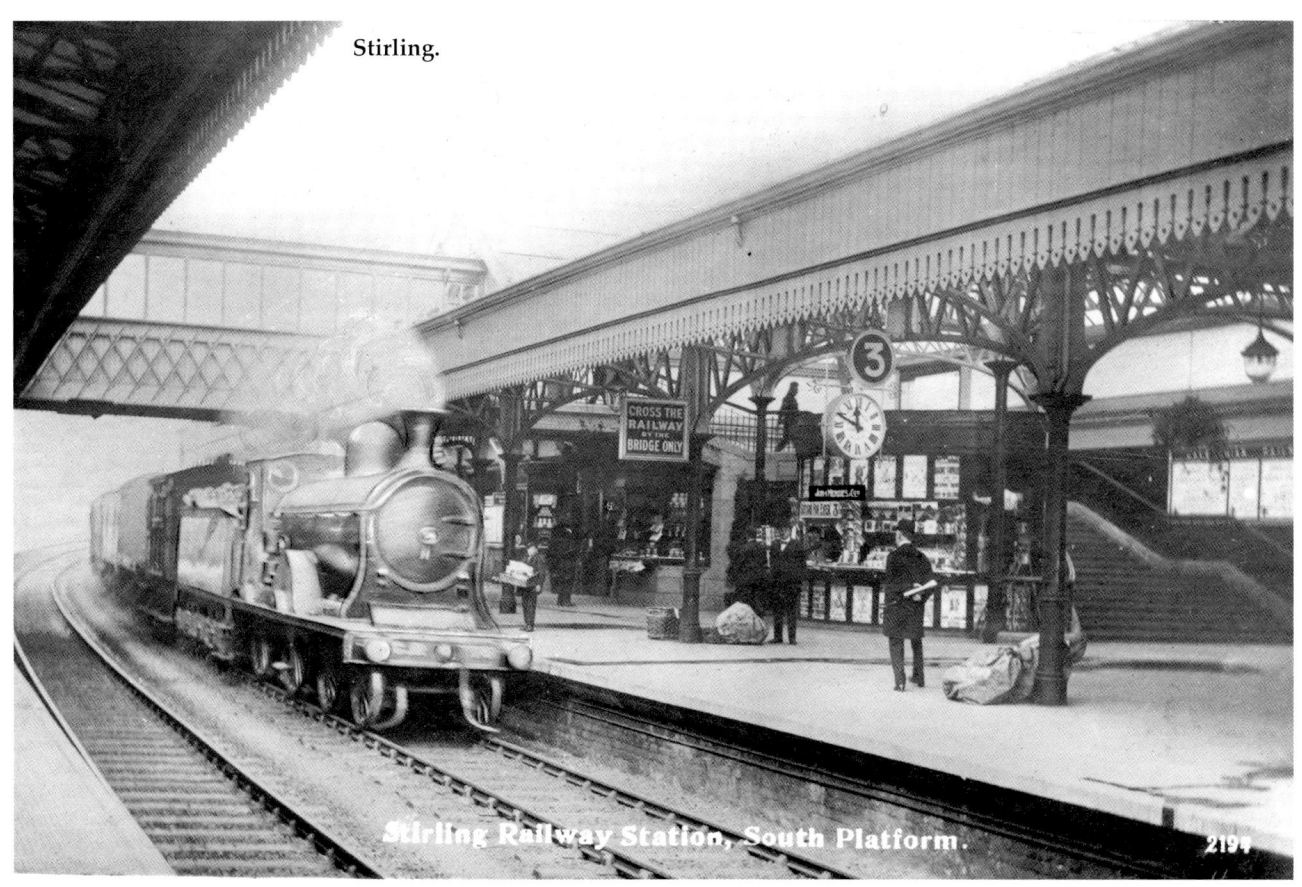

Stirling Railway Station, South Platform.

If there was one merger partner which the Caledonian should have engaged with during the early 1850s – and did not – it was the Edinburgh & Glasgow Railway. This amalgamation (effectively a takeover by the 'Caley') came so close to fruition that the two companies' trade results were bracketed together by the investors' press for many years, and the failure of the two to 'tie the knot' was to create major problems for the Caledonian. In its place, the Edinburgh and Glasgow Railway was to amalgamate with the ambitious North British, thus admitting a major rival into the lucrative travel market in the west of Scotland.

Stirling station.

Dunblane.

The Edinburgh & Glasgow Railway was the 'Liverpool and Manchester' of Scotland. It was the first trunk line built north of the Border, and connected the two major cities from 1842, five years before the Caledonian ran its first train. Running across a narrow isthmus between two important cities, it should have been a high-earning company, but it was not.

Like many railway concerns at the time, the Edinburgh & Glasgow was badly run. Its management was one of the poorest in the country – which was saying something – and its Board had made the nonsensical decision to tackle competition from the waterway system by lowering fares, instead of concentrating on their strength, namely speed, which the two canals (the Forth & Clyde Canal connecting with the Union Canal) could not possibly match.

Dunblane.

Forteviot staff.

Moncrieff tunnel repairs 1901.

Moncrieff tunnel repairs 1901.

On realising that the Edinburgh & Glasgow might be a target for a merger, or even a takeover, the Caledonian began to make overtures around 1850. The new company swiftly began to show that its directors could match any other company's when it came to inexperience, as they struggled to come to terms with the Edinburgh & Glasgow's merger terms – namely that any dividends to shareholders of a unified company should be commensurate with the intensity of the passenger service provided between the cities. As O.S. Nock observed, the Caledonian would have been well-advised to treat this as an opening negotiation gambit, instead of responding to it as a spur. For the 'Caley' decided to enter this near-suicidal rivalry with the Edinburgh & Glasgow and the canals, and began offering its own sixpenny fare on an intensive service frequency between Edinburgh & Glasgow! The idea was to provide the Caledonian directors with a firm base for negotiations, but it was a disastrously expensive way to tackle the problem. To make matters worse, the 'Caley' route was by far the longest between the two cities, since it involved running trains via Carstairs.

Perth.

Denny.

So debilitating was this competition that the company very quickly had to withdraw from it. Not only had this brought in negligible income against considerable outgoings, it also had eroded confidence in the directors' capabilities. Nowhere was this expressed so volubly as in London, and the Caledonian, despite having by 1850 substantially completed its dream of building (and leasing) a main line from the Border to Glasgow, Edinburgh, Dundee, and Aberdeen, now had another crisis in the boardroom.

Airth.

South Alloa.

It was typical of the company that, at a time when its bank overdraft had been stopped at £50,000, the directors got down to the business of choosing designs for staff uniforms, and in particular, deciding the appearance of coat buttons. These were to be silver with a thistle motif in the centre. Interestingly, a museum example illustrated in George Dow's definitive work *Railway Heraldry* (1985 supplement), appears to also incorporate a lion couchant – not quite the Scottish style. The Lord Lyon, King of Arms, has confirmed that the late Mr Dow's book is quite correct in stating that the Caledonian did not receive official permission to adopt the Arms of Scotland as its own device. Technically, the matter could have been raised by the Court's Procurator Fiscal, but in fact no action was taken. One wonders if one of the company's aristocratic backers – perhaps the Duke of Buccleuch – had a quiet word in a royal ear?. The use of the 'wrong' kind of lion is a sure sign that heraldic authority had been bypassed.

The long-term significance of the failure to take over the Edinburgh & Glasgow Railway should not be underestimated. Not only was the NBR, the Caledonian's main rival, given a main line approach into central Glasgow – and from there it was to develop a suburban network north of the Clyde stretching to Loch Lomond, and north-west as far as Mallaig, but also Caledonian trains travelling from Carlisle to Aberdeen would have to pay the NBR for the privilege to do so. Nowadays it is the only section of the Monkland line to remain.

Alloa Swing Bridge.

Locomotives to 1894

87, 2-2-2, built 1865

In 1845 the Caledonian directors decided to order 50 steam locomotives and 400 passenger carriages. By the end of the following year, the proposed locomotive fleet was considered insufficient for both passenger and freight traffic, and a further 30 goods engines were planned, plus three banking engines. The 'Caley' directors certainly could not be faulted for optimism! In contrast, the NBR began with 38 units, a number of which found themselves leased out to the Edinburgh & Glasgow.

Whether such large orders were actually placed is not immediately clear from the Caledonian Board minutes and realism appears to have entered their calculations before long. Fifteen engines and tenders were scheduled to be delivered from the Lancastrian firm of Jones and Potts by the summer of 1847 (at a cost of £2,200 each), with a later order being placed with a firm called Charles Tayleur, better known in later years as the Vulcan Foundry. By the summer of 1846 only 35 carriages were under construction, indicating that the Directors were now coming to grips with the realities of building a major highway between England and Scotland.

100, 2-4-0, at Barnhill (Perth), built 1867

248, 0-4-2, built 1864.

436, 2-4-0, built 1867.

Unlike the North British, the Caledonian leased neighbouring lines' engines from the start, four locomotives from the Garnkirk and the Greenock systems being utilised in early operations. After taking over those companies, the Caledonian inherited three from the former and fifteen from the latter, as well as three from the Polloc & Govan and ten from the Wishaw & Coltness. By contrast, the North British began with its own, Newcastle-built units, if only because its only absorbed rival, the Edinburgh and Dalkeith, had no engines to offer (apart from a stationary unit in Edinburgh), being literally horse-powered.

The Caledonian's first Locomotive Superintendent was Robert Sinclair who did his best to assimilate this varied fleet of engines, but who reportedly found his Board difficult to work with. In particular he was frustrated at having to build more singles for express work, instead of his own preference for 2-4-0s. A single was a locomotive with a single pair of powered driving wheels, often of considerable diameter. One such, the famous No. 123 of 1896, was to become the company's totem, and probably its best-remembered locomotive of all.

1167, 0-4-4 built 1873.

By 1856 Sinclair had had enough of the 'Caley' and took an appointment with the Eastern Counties Railway. He was replaced by Benjamin Conner, who began work in new workshops at St Rollox in Glasgow, replacing Greenock as the principal plant for the company. Conner (so spelt in the company records) was to hold the position for 20 years, only McIntosh running him close in terms of longevity of service.

Conner had no inhibition about singles, soon undertaking the construction of a class of '8 footers'. These carried the distinctive louvred splashers which identified the Caledonian so closely with its southern partner, continuing the design standards of Alexander Allan, who had moved north from the LNWR to the Scottish Central. These '8 footers', whose driving wheel diameters actually varied between 98 and 100 inches, held sway on Anglo-Scottish expresses for the best part of 30 years. They were still being built in the mid-1870s, (when the North British had begun to construct 4-4-0s) and were still pulling their weight at the end of the century.

127, 4-4-0 built 1876.

30, 2-4-0, built 1872 at Larbert.

The weight they could pull was limited compared to a locomotive with four driving wheels, and of considerably smaller diameter. With carriage weights increasing, the Caledonian could no longer rely on sprightly singles with limited adhesion, and double-heading on express services was becoming increasingly common in the 1870s, despite the introduction of 2-4-0 designs in 1865 and again two years later. Something bigger was required, and the 'Caley' could hardly failed to note that its rival, the NBR, was working into Carlisle with 4-4-0s, courtesy of Wheatley and Drummond. This was a sufficient spur for change!

In 1876 Conner retired after 20 years service, being replaced by George Brittain. He had five 4-4-0s running within the year, but these appeared to have been 'under-boilered' and could not match the singles for speed. A more successful class with this wheel arrangement was the 'Oban Bogie', a later 4-4-0 design, introduced in 1882 for service on the steeply-graded Callander & Oban line. To modern eyes, these engines look 'under-boilered' as well, but worked on the line for the best part of a quarter of a century before being retired to less demanding parts of the system, some members of the class lasting into the late 1920s (although only after rebuilding by McIntosh).

147, 2-4-0T built 1879.

72, 4-4-0, built 1884, rebuilt 1903, after an accident at Greenloaning

The appointment of Dugald Drummond in August 1882 was a sign that the Caledonian intended to dominate the Scottish railway scene. Not only was Drummond already renowned for his express locomotives on the North British, his recruitment from this, the company's leading rival, showed the 'Caley' directors' determination to master their enemy company by weakening it as well as adding to their own strength. It was as if Rangers had persuaded Jock Stein to leave Celtic for Ibrox!

Drummond was already known for his 'Abbotsford' 4-4-0s – and for other things as well, being reputedly hot-tempered, with no worries about being unpopular with underlings!. The 'Abbotsfords' were built for the NBR's Waverley Route and were described by contemporary railway expert, Professor Foxwell, as putting up performances on the new Midland Railway & NBR joint trains, that were unequalled anywhere in the world. This is a measure of Drummond's reputation, although interestingly, he began his career at St. Rollox by designing a goods 0-6-0.

354, 0-6-0 built 1884.

This became very much the standard-bearer of CR freight operations in the decades to come. Known as 'Jumbos', there were 244 of these engines, with additional marques being built by later designers. Although ostensibly intended for freight duties, and entirely suitable for these, later members of Drummond's class were fitted with Westinghouse brake for passenger duties; indeed, some were fitted with condensing apparatus to allow them to work on suburban trains through the new low level line in Glasgow. One unwelcome addition was the fitting of stovepipe chimneys to many of these, and other, Caledonian engines in later years.

Drummond was better known for his 4-4-0s and he produced two classes for the Caledonian over the years 1884-8. His first comprised 29 engines with 78 inch diameter driving wheels, for express work throughout the system. He followed this with a class of twelve with 69 inch wheels for the Greenock line.

123, 4-2-2 built 1886.

Curiously, in view of his expertise in designing express locomotives with a leading bogie and four driving wheels, Drummond also produced a 'one off' single. This was none other than No. 123, a 4-2-2 built by the Neilson Company in Glasgow, ostensibly for the 1886 International Exhibition in Edinburgh, but carrying an unmistakable Drummond stamp.

On this one engine, the Caledonian's prestige depended when the first Race to the North broke out in that year. More detail appears in the chapter 'Racing Days', but the decision of operational management to entrust a racing train to a single – when Beattock and Cobbinshaw Banks had to be climbed against the clock – was a surprising one. No. 123 didn't let the company down and she set a standard for excellence in express working that the Caledonian would never lose.

123 in her LMS guise of 14010.

Biggar.

Biggar.

Broughton.

Stobo.

At Peebles, the Caledonian Railway station is near the bridge over the River Tweed. The viaduct that carried the railway to the rival NBR station can be seen on the left hand edge of the photograph.

Peebles station from the Tweed bridge.

Dolphinton.

Drumelzier, looking south up Tweeddale. The Symington Peebles branch is just visible in the foreground.

Water Schemes

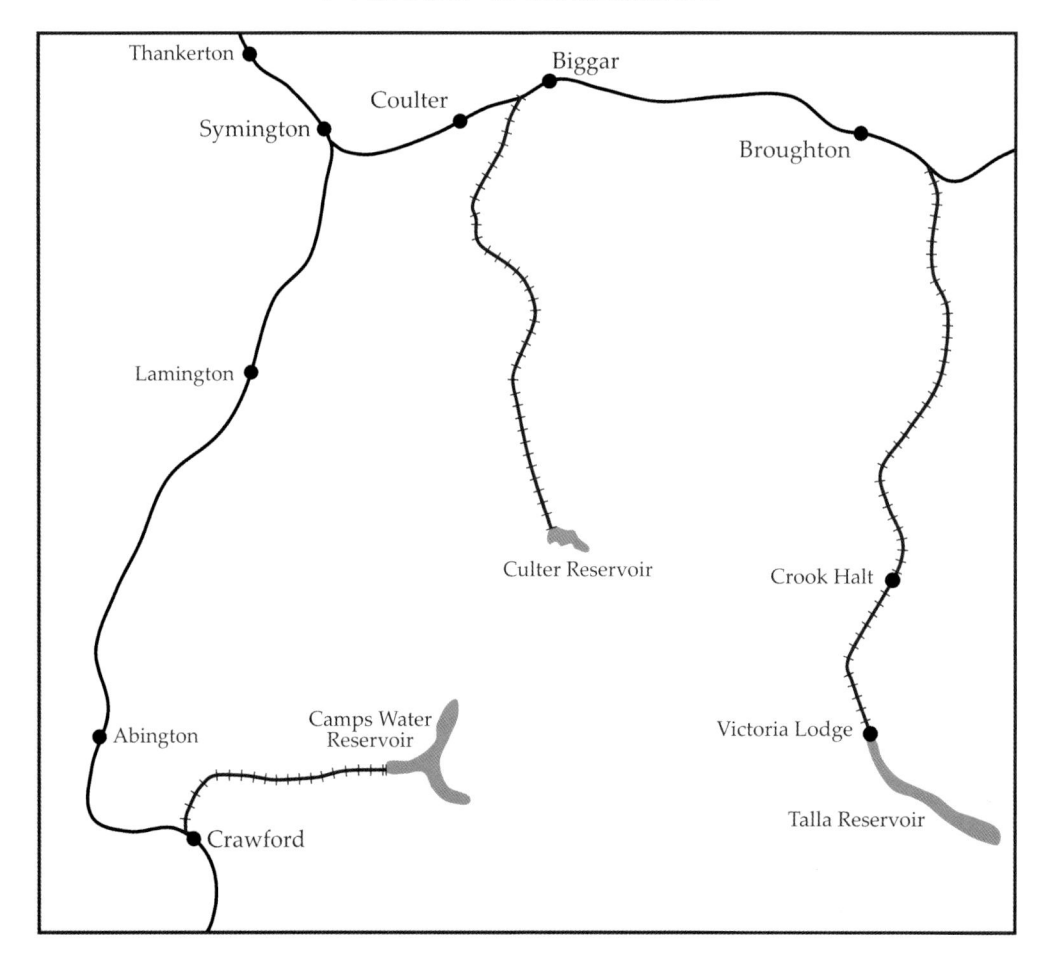

Construction work on the Talla Reservoir dam. The foundations for the Victoria Lodge are on the left.

The Talla railway was one of a number of water projects that used the Caledonian Railway to provide a base from which a private railway was built into the hills to the construction site of a reservoir. It is without doubt also the best known of the these. The reservoir itself was built to provide water to Edinburgh, the aqueduct from it stretches northwards for thirty miles to the Glencorse reservoir in the Pentland hills. The railway to the dam site was about eight miles long and branched off the Symington and Peebles line south into Tweeddale, crossing the Biggar water at Rachan Home Farm (the buildings visible in the foreground of the photograph opposite). A light railway followed the line of the aqueduct north towards Edinburgh. The first sod was cut in 1895 and the railway reached the dam site in 1897 almost exactly two years later. For the next eight years the line saw traffic until the opening of the reservoir on 28 September 1905. After the opening the railway was effectively closed despite local intrest in maintaining the rail link, the rails were offered for sale in 1910 and they were lifted two years later.

View towards the Victoria Lodge from the top of the dam.

Construction of the bridge over the spillway of the dam.

Special trains bringing guests for the opening.

The opening ceremony of the Talla Reservoir, at the Victoria Lodge adjacent to the dam. The opening of the reservoir was carried out by Lady Cranston, the wife of the Lord Provost of Edinburgh. The Victoria Lodge itself was built to house a boardroom for the trustees of the Edinburgh and District Water Trust during the construction of the reservoir, and to house their staff who oversaw the project. One other poigniant reminder of the endevour is to be found in the graveyard of the Tweedsmuir Church, where a memorial stone stands dedicated to the thirty men who lost their lives during the construction and were buried there.

One of Robert McAlpine's engines leaving the sidings at Causewayend, Biggar.

In 1903 a project to supply water to Motherwell was begun and a railway laid to bring in material from a junction near Biggar. The railway ran parallel to the present A702 past Culter Allers farm then up the Culter Water into the hills to the Culter waterhead where the dam was constructed. The village at Waterhead was well supplied with a school, a mission house and reading room. The reservoir was completed in 1907 in spite of the weather which had caused significant difficulties, frequent delays were caused by heavy snowfall and hard frost which made working with both concrete and clay impossible

Waterhead village with the earthworks of the dam rising in the background.

Clearing snow at Douglas.

Construction of the viaduct that carried the railway across the Clyde to the site of the reservoir.

Site of the reservoir, looking east, the prisoner of war camp on the right hand side.

Exit of the tunnel that carries the aqueduct near Abington.

Excavations for the dam embankment looking north.

In May 1914 the Standing Joint Comittee of Lanarkshire gave their consent to the construction of the Camps Reservoir, to feed the growing demand for water in the Motherwell and Hamilton area. A construction railway was started from a point near Crawford station to the site of the reservoir. As a result of the project beginning during the First World War considerable labour shortages were encountered. To overcome the shortages the services of 200 prisoners of war were obtained from the War Office. It was stipulated by the war office that the prisoners had to be paid the standard rate for their labour and must not be used near or on the main road or be permitted to use explosives. In spite of the restrictions the POW completed much of the work on the railway and access roads to the reservoir site and the excavation required for the dam. Shortly after the Armistice prisoner of war labour was dispensed with and British workmen carried out the work until the reservoir opened in 1930. The access railway was lifted shortly afterwards.

The Camps dam nearing completion.

Crossing the Solway

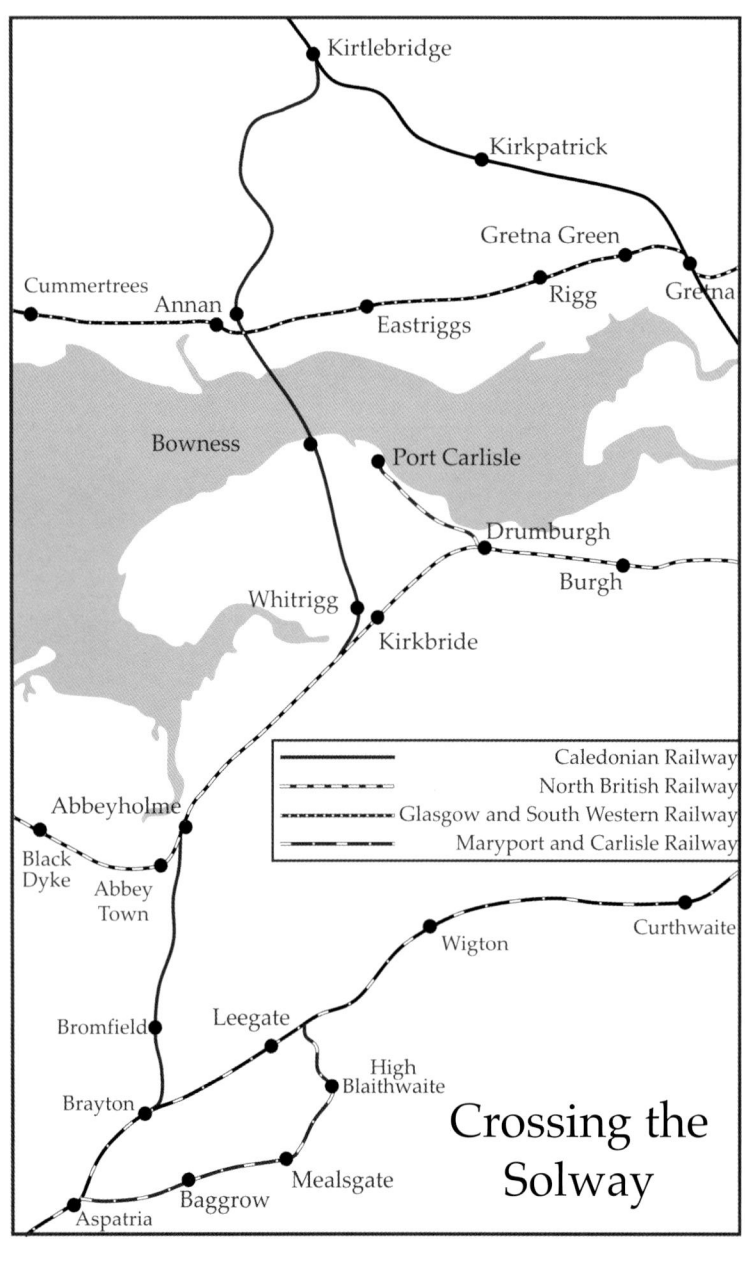

Solway viaduct.

Kirtlebridge, the line to the viaduct diverges to the left of the photograph.

Railways crossed the Anglo-Scottish Border at no fewer than seven places at one time. Four of these frontier crossings were located on dry land, two crossed a river, but only one connected England and Scotland by a bridge over salt water – the Caledonian's Solway crossing.

This is a measure of the uniqueness of the Solway Junction Railway, whose centrepiece was a 1,900 yard viaduct running across the Solway Firth from near Annan in Dumfriesshire to Bowness in what is now Cumbria. It was the longest bridge in Europe when built in 1869, although it was soon to be eclipsed by the Tay Bridge.

The Solway Viaduct was designed by Thomas Brunlees, a Kelso engineer who actually specialised in piers – the record-breaking Southend Pier is one of his. Of no great height (35 feet above low water), the Solway Viaduct had no outstanding feature, apart from the use of gimlet-pointed supports to accelerate the sinking of the 193 columns.

A single line was carried across the firth, there being an early problem when it appeared that the Board of Trade might require an opening span to allow traffic up to Port Carlisle. The promoters bought off this expensive possibility by persuading the Port Carlisle traders to admit that their harbour had no commercial future. Presumably they required some compensation before being persuaded! The North British, newly-installed in this tiny Cumbrian port, helpfully announced that they would not require an opening section – but they had plans to see their trains crossing the firth.

Looking across the Solway along the length of the viaduct from Bowness.

The construction of the bridge took less time than that of the line over Bowness Moss immediately to the south. When finished, this latter stretch of line failed a Board of Trade inspection – something that rarely happened in the history of Britain's railways before the collapse of the first Tay Bridge.

Thus it was not the Caledonian Railway which was responsible for spanning the Solway. The Solway Junction Railway Company had been established in 1864 by a consortium of West Cumbrian ironmasters who were anxious to speed up the delivery of haematite ore, production of which had increased seven times over in the previous seven years, to the foundries of Lanarkshire, avoiding the bottleneck of Carlisle.

Bowness on Solway.

This was an ambitious plan for promoters not exclusively interested in transport, but the project began to assume a life of its own when it became clear that none of the four companies nearby – the Maryport & Carlisle Railway and the NBR in England, the CR and the GSWR in Scotland – could afford to ignore a development which might avail a business opportunity for a rival company. The iron masters cleverly negotiated exchange facilities with the Maryport & Carlisle at Brayton, running-powers over part of the NBR Silloth Branch, and more exchange facilities with both the GSWR at Annan, and the 'Caley' at Kirtlebridge on the West Coast Main Line. This was a bet well-hedged!

Although we look back on the Solway Viaduct as carrying a Caledonian line, the North British was so interested in the Solway Junction Railway in the late 1860s that it opened negotiations with the new company about installing NBR staff at Annan Station (later Annan Shawhill), while Annan itself was listed in a parliamentary document in 1865 as an exchange point for traffic between the NBR and GSWR.

However, when the Solway Junction Railway directors began to experience financial difficulties – and early traffic returns were disappointing – the NBR was in something of a fiscal crisis itself, and the Caledonian hurriedly stepped in, securing an agreement to work the Solway line from its opening in 1869. The GSWR seems to have lost out again to its bigger Glasgow rival, but in view of the problems which the Solway was to cause, perhaps the "Sou' West" was well out of it. The Caledonian's company records show that it supplied locomotives and crews from the outset, based initially at Kirtlebridge, although there appears to have been a small shed at Brayton as well.

Kirkbride Junction.

Bromfield.

By 1880 it was possible for a passenger to leave Edinburgh Princes Street at 2.25 in the afternoon, or 2.15 from Glasgow Central and, after changing at Kirtlebridge, be at Bowness before 6 pm. This journey would include a sea crossing, which in bad weather could doubtless be rather too exciting! One older resident of the area recalled that crossing the Solway Viaduct was like being on a boat, particularly when the tide was high. A 20-foot tide, combined with wind-whipped waves would have left little leeway between train and sea.

One of the least developed of Britain's estuaries, the Solway can often present a peaceful aspect, with Scottish residents treated to views of Skiddaw and Blencathra in good weather, while those on the English side have a fine view of Criffel. But in winter the Solway is a completely different animal, as both the Solway Junction Railway and the Caledonian were soon to discover.

In January 1881 no fewer than 45 of the viaduct's supports and 37 of its girders collapsed because of the pressure of ice flows on the firth. One of them was 27 yards square and six feet thick. Has any other British railway had to close because of what was essentially pack ice? No train was able to cross the Solway for the next three years.

Brayton Junction.

The Caledonian Board was remarkably unsympathetic to the Cumbrian businessmen who had worked so hard to make the line a reality. An offer to sell the line to them was treated with contempt by the CR directors, who instead demanded compensation from their wretched Solway counterparts for lack of income from their working agreement. Eventually, a new Act of Parliament was necessary before enough finance could be generated to allow major repairs to be carried out, including the addition of flanges sharp enough to break any more ice (and there was more in 1886). Not surprisingly, the Solway Junction Railway could barely struggle on much longer as an independent entity, and it merged with the Caledonian in 1895.

This was purely a nominal arrangement, the 'Caley' now taking over a line which it never particularly wanted or needed in the first place. Maintenance was reduced to the extent that the viaduct was considered unsafe during World War One, and closure took place in 1921. The Solway Junction Company, by then existing formally at a business address in the Isle of Wight, was not even notified about the viaduct's closure! Passenger traffic continued on the northern end of the line (Kirtlebridge-Annan) for another ten years. Annan Shawhill Station had been listed as 'Annan 1' for many years in the local telephone directory, so it had stolen a march on the GSWR station, even if only temporarily.

It was a sad end to a noble, if muddle-headed, venture. But muddle continued to feature in the viaduct's story. In the early 1930s, the LMS decided to demolish it, but, based in faraway Glasgow, the company officials failed to carry out the consultations required with the local authorities and the Crown Estate Commissioners and cheerfully authorised the use of dynamite to remove the supports – this in an estuary famous for its salmon. Much of the remaining demolition work had to be undertaken by hand, resulting in the deaths of three workers and the threat of lawsuits from local fishermen.

Nowadays the Solway appears almost as pristine as when the engineers first attempted to span it with iron. Only the stone approach embankments at Annan and Bowness, and the fragile tracery of cast iron piers at the latter point, testify to a forgotten chapter of Caledonian Railway history.

Wanlockhead.

Between Wanlockhead and Leadhills.

Leadhills.

Leadhills.

64

Glenbuck, the Spireslack branch in background

Coalburn.

Viaduct over the Clyde, near Lanark.

Underground and Overground

Underground in Glasgow, overground in Edinburgh. This was the curious contrast for new Caledonian urban lines in Scotland's two largest cities in the last two decades of the 19th century. In the case of Glasgow, an underground line was built, and still exists, while in Edinburgh an even more grandiose scheme failed to flourish.

Although traditionally regarded as a Glasgow company, the Caledonian was pre-empted in the building of a cross-city underground line by both the NBR and the cable-operated Underground. In the form of the Glasgow City and District line, the NBR had ambitiously built at right angles under its Queen Street terminus and provided a passenger service along the north bank of the Clyde, linking Bellgrove – or farther afield – with a link to the west as far as Loch Lomond. It was unthinkable that the Caledonian could not do as least as well.

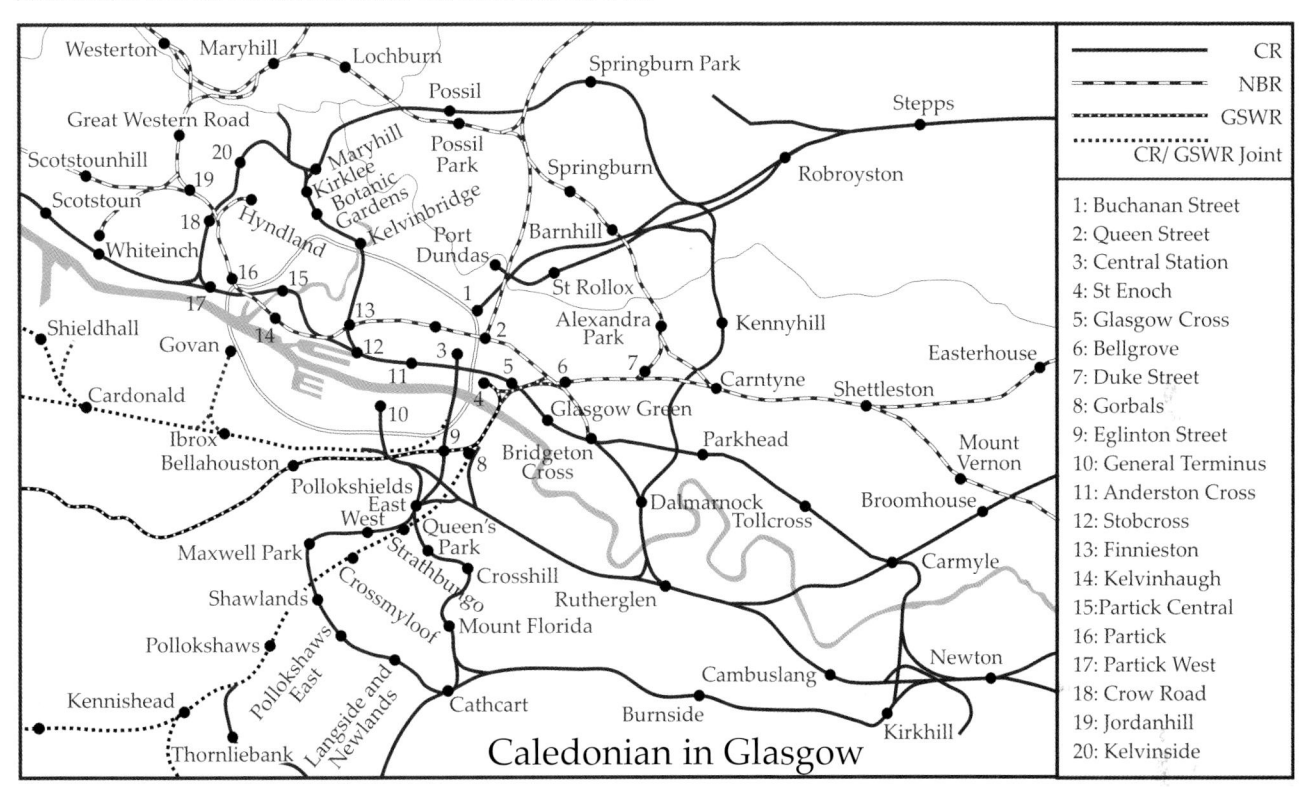

Caledonian in Glasgow

Key:
- CR
- NBR
- GSWR
- CR/GSWR Joint

1: Buchanan Street
2: Queen Street
3: Central Station
4: St Enoch
5: Glasgow Cross
6: Bellgrove
7: Duke Street
8: Gorbals
9: Eglinton Street
10: General Terminus
11: Anderston Cross
12: Stobcross
13: Finnieston
14: Kelvinhaugh
15: Partick Central
16: Partick
17: Partick West
18: Crow Road
19: Jordanhill
20: Kelvinside

Glasgow Cross.

Partick Central.

Distracted by the need to rationalise and modernise its main line approach through Bridge Street to Central Station, the Caledonian was slow to embark on an underground line. Indeed, its earliest plans for a line along the north bank were for an elevated railway, plans which simultaneously created fears for the destruction of existing streets and buildings, as well as dreams of avarice for what financial claims could be made against the company.

An underground line was an obvious alternative, although not a particularly cheaper one. The Glasgow Central Railway was opened on 10 August 1896, linking Rutherglen by running along the north bank of the Clyde, through a new low level Central Station, with the Stobcross Dock area and destinations even farther west. Within the city, Maryhill could be reached, and Possil was also joined to the network.

A class of 4-4-0 tanks was introduced by John Lambie to operate the new services, and these were fitted with condensing apparatus intended to minimise pollution from smoke and steam. These were soon joined by a class of ten condensing 0-4-4Ts, and members of the earlier class eventually found their way to more pastoral surroundings, one of them surviving to 1938. The 0-4-4T design was destined to be even longer-lasting, one example being preserved on the Bo'ness and Kinneil Railway.

Kelvinbridge.

Maryhill.

The Glasgow line's arrival was stalked by the new electric tram services which provided cheaper fares and a greater frequency. Historian John Thomas wrote of the trams being ominously audible overhead to passengers standing on the new low level platforms. But at least the Caledonian had done its best for its native city, providing a north bank route that might well have been considered as an alternative to a Clyde crossing for main line trains to and from the south, and making possible the concept of one super Central – not necessarily a terminus – also handling services to Edinburgh, Dundee and Aberdeen, instead of Buchanan Street. But a suburban service was better than allowing the intrusive NBR to have things all its own way on the north bank and gave the 'Caley' access to the important Stobcross Docks.

This cross-Glasgow line succumbed to closure in 1964 – on the face of it, a curious fate for a public transport facility in a city which has found it necessary to blast motorways through its heart to accommodate car use. Perhaps the travelling public was simply fed up with the dirt and condensation of the underground stations, and it is noticeable that the Central Low Level Station was built in tunnel, unlike its Queen Street counterpart, which, although dingy, had platform ends in the open air. Surely early electrification would have been the solution, but the former 'Caley' line closed on 5 October 1964, around five years after the former NBR line was electrified. Fortunately, much of the route was reopened as the Argyle Street line on 1 November 1979. There had been nothing wrong with the concept; it was the motive power – steam – that was the problem.

Maryhill, the Kelvin Aqueduct and Dawsholm gasworks are behind the train.

Mount Florida.

A more conventional suburban railway which has served Glasgow well, for more than a century now, is the Cathcart Circle. This is a six-mile loop from a junction 1 miles out of Central and running through the city's southern suburbs and back to Pollokshields. Like so many extensions to the Caledonian network after 1860, the Cathcart District Railway Company was a 'proxy' railway. Researchers examining the company archives will find that the first meeting of the directors took place in a solicitor's office in West Regent Street on 16 December 1880. Only two men described themselves as promoters at that time – George Browne, Provost of Crosshill and accountant William Giffen Lindsay – but an enabling Act of Parliament was already on the statute book, and it is not long before references to the Caledonian Railway begin to make their appearance in the Minutes.

The area encircled was by no means urbanised at that time, but the Caledonian knew a good investment when it saw one and was anxious in any event to prevent GSWR expansion in the area. Not surprisingly, the CR put up half the capital and operated the line at cost. The Cathcart District Railway itself lasted until 1923 as an independent company, being taken over by the LMS six months earlier than the Caledonian itself.

Clarkston.

Busby Station from the road.

BUSBY RAILWAY STATION.

At one time, there was a train every ten minutes on the Cathcart Circle, a frequency unequalled anywhere else outside London. As well as converting rural south Glasgow into a kind of Metroland, the Cathcart Circle also served the national football stadium, Hampden Park, accessible from Mount Florida Station, and trains could be run directly there from other parts of the system.

The line was operated mainly by 0-4-4 tanks, until superseded by more modern 2-6-4Ts in late LMS and early BR days. Polmadie Shed often employed its largest express engines on 'filling-in' turns on the line before 1923, and when the first 4–6–0s had been introduced on to the main line in 1902, it was the only way to turn them, such was their length.

Thorntonhall

Surprisingly, there was no move towards more up-to-date power, until electrification was promised in 1956, although it took another six years, including four years of DMU operation, before the 'Blue Trains' began operating round the loop. Nowadays, the Cathcart Circle remains a vital part of the Glasgow transport infrastructure. It can also claim to be one of the few railways to be named in the title of a novel – *Snooker Tam of the Cathcart Railway*, written by R.W. Campbell and published in 1919.

Edinburgh's overground line was built – at great expense – although to be accurate there would also have been a subterranean element to it, had the City Fathers approved. In 1890 the Caledonian seriously proposed building an extension eastwards from its Princes Street terminus, under the length of Princes Street, plunging through the heart of the volcanic Calton Hill and surfacing again in the Lochend area of the city. Here the line would diverge, one route heading northwards to Seafield and South Leith, the other turning west and crossing the rooftops of Leith to reach the existing branch from Princes Street in a triangular junction at Newhaven.

So abhorrent was the prospect of vents in the middle of Princes Street that the city authorities entered into a pact with the North British Railway which, as it happens, was hoping to double its existing track through Princes Street Gardens. By accepting a NBR proposal of a surface line to Leith from Abbeyhill – a line the company really didn't want – the city gave its blessing to a second Haymarket tunnel being built to parallel the bore made by the Edinburgh & Glasgow Railway some 50 years earlier, and also permitted the single Mound bore to become three.

EAST KILBRIDE

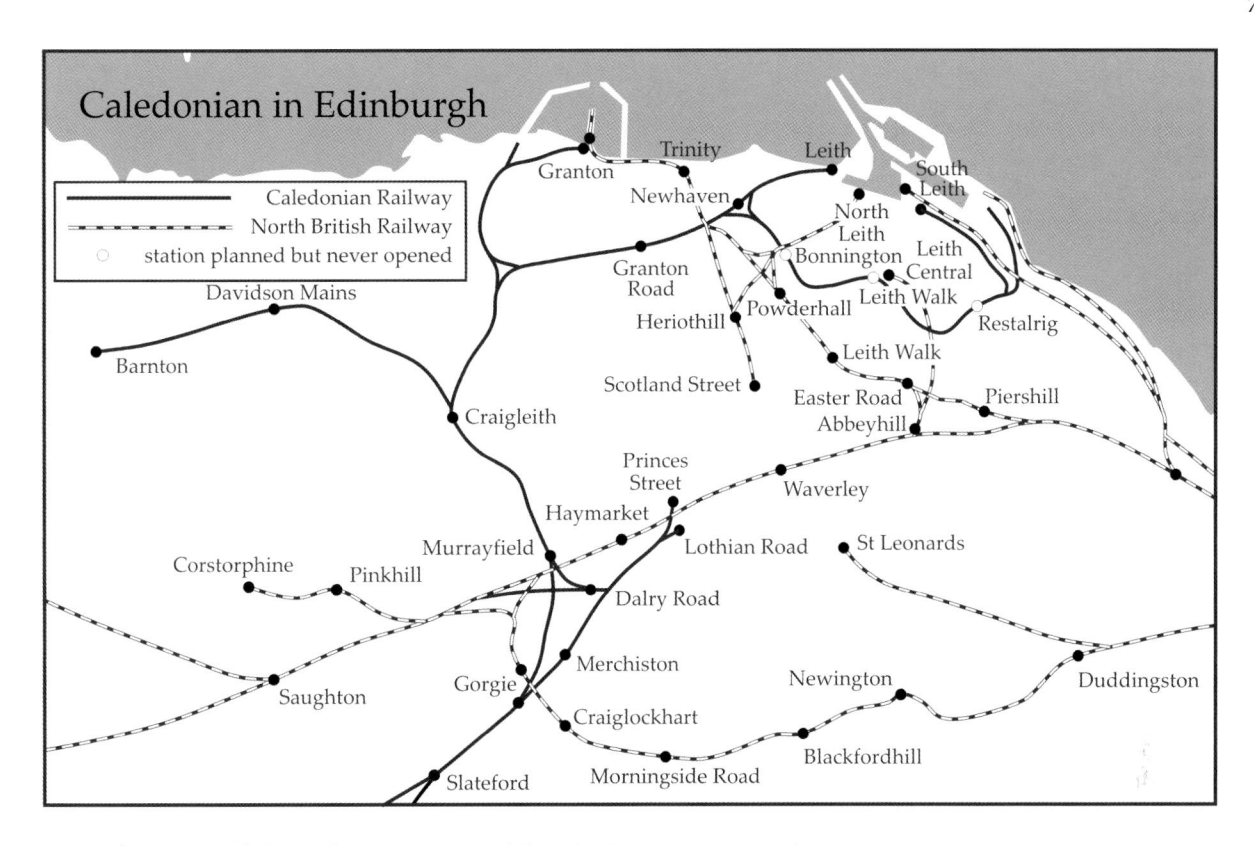

Caledonian in Edinburgh

— Caledonian Railway
–•–•– North British Railway
○ station planned but never opened

Barnton — Davidson Mains — Craigleith — Granton — Trinity — Newhaven — Granton Road — Heriothill — Scotland Street — Powderhall — Bonnington — North Leith — Leith — South Leith — Leith Central — Leith Walk — Restalrig — Easter Road — Abbeyhill — Piershill — Princes Street — Haymarket — Waverley — Corstorphine — Pinkhill — Murrayfield — Lothian Road — St Leonards — Dalry Road — Saughton — Gorgie — Merchiston — Newington — Duddingston — Slateford — Craiglockhart — Morningside Road — Blackfordhill

Granton Harbour.

Cross-Leith line in the 1940s.

This effectively stymied the Caledonian proposal to reach Leith from the east, the parliamentarians of 1890 merely granting the company authority to go ahead with its cross-Leith line from Newhaven, which would have formed the northern half of this proposed circle. In the circumstances it was surprising that the line went ahead at all, particularly in view of the amount of property clearance and bridgework involved. Stations were even partially laid out at Ferry Road, Bonnington and off Leith Walk.

It may have taken a little time for the company's directors to realise that, by agreeing to Leith Town Council's requirement that their fare would be pegged to that of the NBR with its shorter Central line, they would be running services for a ridiculously low return on a much longer route. They could not even use rival tram services as an excuse for revenue loss; although Leith operated electric trams from 1904, journeys to Edinburgh were interrupted at Pilrig, as the capital used cable traction.

Redford Cavalry Barracks near Colinton.

If passenger trains were non-existent, even freight traffic was light; by 1917 the line was operated only as a single line branch. By 1920 the loco depot at its eastern end, at Seafield, was leased to its triumphant enemy, the NBR, secure in its lair. This author never saw any locomotives on this line of CR or LMS design, only former NBR 0-6-0s.

The Caledonian could have rescued something from the wreckage of this Act by turning its new Leith Walk Goods Station into passenger use. It was only yards from the bustle of Leith Walk itself, surrounded by a tenemental population, and with two lengthy platforms for Leith-Glasgow trains, had they been required. But it was not to be. Edinburgh's only "Caley" suburban passenger services were from Princes Street to Balerno, Barnton, and to Leith.

But perhaps the Caledonian had the last laugh after all; its Leith Station at Lindsay Road outlasted three NBR termini. Indeed the 1962 closure of the Leith North terminus was controversial, being effected just as two high-rise blocks of flats took shape only yards away. This seemed to sum up a century of Caledonian operations in Edinburgh – bursts of over-ambitious activity made without reference to actual transport requirements.

Juniper Green.

Balerno.

High Blantyre.

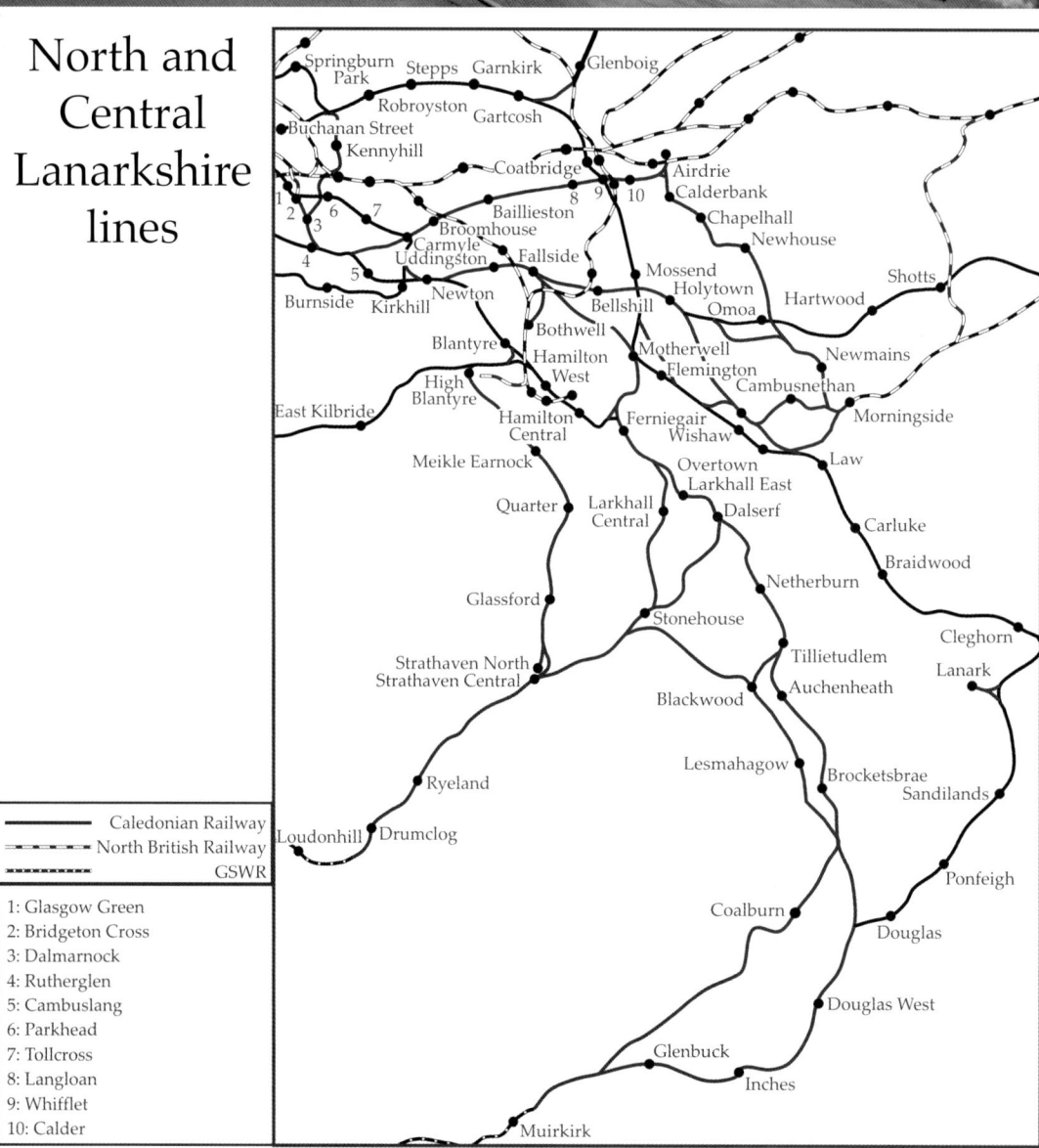

North and Central Lanarkshire lines

Caledonian Railway
North British Railway
GSWR

1: Glasgow Green
2: Bridgeton Cross
3: Dalmarnock
4: Rutherglen
5: Cambuslang
6: Parkhead
7: Tollcross
8: Langloan
9: Whifflet
10: Calder

Glassford.

Strathaven North.

Hamilton Central at street level.

Platforms of Hamilton Central.

Larkhall Central.

Viaduct over the Avon, Larkhall

Viaduct at Stonehouse.

Stonehouse.

Pomillion Viaducts, Strathaven.

The Central Station, Strathaven

Dalserf.

Tillietudlem.

Blackwood.

New Station, Lesmahagow.

1831 GLASGOW TO COATBRIDGE 8 MILES

1904 GLASGOW (CENTRAL) TO LONDON (EUSTON) 401 MILES
CORRIDOR TRAIN LEAVING GLASGOW (CENTRAL)

1904 CORRIDOR TRAIN PASSING OVER BEATTOCK SUMMIT

1831. Glasgow to Coatbridge 8 miles.

1906. Corridor Train passing over Beattock Summit

EARLIEST GARNKIRK (NOW CALEDONIAN) ENGINE, 1831—GEO. STEPHENSON, 11 TONS.

CALEDONIAN ENGINE, NO. 50, 128 TONS (NOW RUNNING ON 2 P.M. CORRIDOR TRAIN FROM GLASGOW, CENTRAL, TO LONDON, EUSTON).

CALEDONIAN SPECIAL TRAIN CONVEYING PAPER FOR GLASGOW, EVENING NEWS

ENGINE 17.
END OF RECORD RUN, LONDON (EUSTON) TO ABERDEEN.
JOHN SOUTER, DRIVER, EXAMINING HIS ENGINE ON ARRIVAL,
23rd AUGUST, 1895.

ON CALEDONIAN RAILWAY.
CORRIDOR COMPOSITE BRAKE CARRIAGE.

DINING SALOON (TABLES SET FOR DINNER).

Grampian Corridor Express Passing Stonehaven.   CALEDONIAN RAILWAY.

LOCKERBIE STATION.

Caledonian Railway Station, Motherwell.

THE STATION, CAMBUSLANG

Eglinton Street Glasgow.

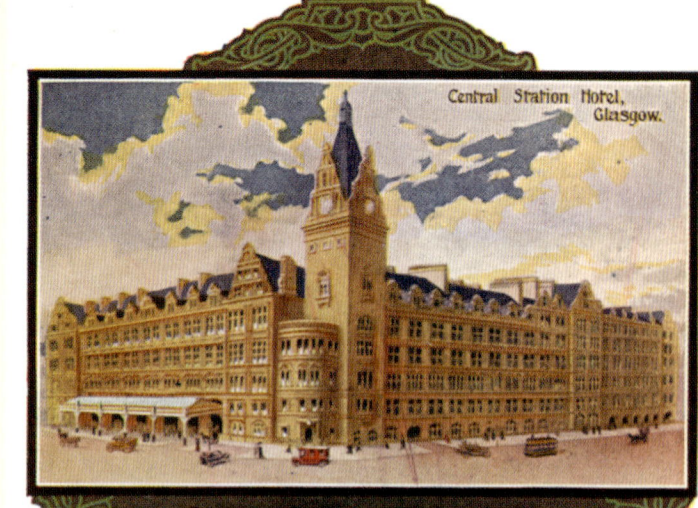

Central Railway Station, Glasgow, Coast Platforms

Central Station, Glasgow.

Central Station Hotel, Glasgow.

CALEDONIAN RAILWAY COMPANY'S HOTELS

Caledonian Station Hotel, Edinburgh.

West Coast Express at Edinburgh (Princes Street).

Blackford from the North

CRIEFF JUNCTION STATION, AUCHTERARDER.

Perth from Barnhill.

Railway Crossing, Carnoustie.

Railway Viaduct, Marykirk

Railway Station. Laurencekirk.

Railway Station, Drumlithie

Oban Express.

Railway Station and Ben Cruachan, Taynuilt

Oban Station.

Connel Bridge, near Oban — Second Longest Clear Span Railway Bridge in Europe. Total Cost, £100,000. Length of Span, 600 feet.

THE STATION ALMONDBANK

43245
Barnton Station and Burgess Golf Club House, Cramond

Lesmahagow

The Three Viaducts, Strathaven

INTERIOR WEMYSS BAY STATION.

GOUROCK PIER.

Duchess of Hamilton

Duchess of Hamilton dining saloon

Duchess of Hamilton saloon.

THE DINING-ROOM
PRINCES ST. STATION HOTEL
EDINBURGH

Central Station, Glasgow.

Callander & Oban

The modern visitor to Oban, standing in McCaig's Folly overlooking Oban Bay to Kerrera and Mull beyond, gains only a peripheral impression of how the railway changed this most attractive of Scottish towns. While always an important port, especially for traffic to and from the Inner Hebrides, Oban is, even now, many miles from the nearest motorway. It was the railway which made its reputation as a visitor centre.

Rails still enter Oban, but the railway presence here is minuscule compared to that of years gone by. The station has two platform edges, compared to the five of yesteryear, there are no tracks on to the pier (now no more than a quayside jutting into Oban Bay at an angle, offering two docking places) and no locomotive depot. But the trains still run, there is a new station building (like a glorified chip-shop it has to be said) and the line itself musters some of the UK's finest scenery to be seen from a train.

Oban in the 1840s.

Strictly speaking, the Caledonian Railway Company never entered the north-west of Scotland. The nearest points of its system were north Clydeside, or Callander itself. For the line to Oban was built by an independent company, the Callander & Oban Railway, one which was merged into the London Midland & Scottish in 1923, around the same time as the 'Caley'. The Caledonian was responsible for operations on the Callander & Oban and appointed five directors on to its Board. But no reader of this book would expect even the briefest of description of the Caledonian history to be complete without some mention of the line to Oban.

Oban, *circa* 1900.

Ballachulish.

Callander.

Like the West Highland line to Fort William, the Callander & Oban was the child of local agitation for a railway link to the rest of the British transport system. It was fathered by the Scottish Central Railway in 1864, and the latter's links with the Caledonian, plus suspicion of the NBR negotiating running-powers into Callander, ensured that the Caledonian would be forced to become involved in using that attractive town as a railhead to the north or west.

Only days after the Scottish Central Railway had bound itself to the fledgling company attempting to reach Oban by rail (and obtaining an Act of Parliament in July 1865), the larger company was amalgamated with the Caledonian. The Caledonian Railway took over the Scottish Central Railway's assets and liabilities, but the future of the Oban line was by no means assured when placed at the tender mercy of the Caledonian, preoccupied both with consolidating its newly-acquired main line all the way from the Border to Aberdeen, and developing its burgeoning mineral business in Central Scotland. But if the 'Caley' hoped to put its new acquisition on the 'back burner', it reckoned without a certain John Anderson.

Anderson had held an administrative position with the Edinburgh and Glasgow Railway, and appears to have lost his job in the takeover by the North British in 1865. The NBR would have done well to have kept him on, and could have prevented Caledonian Blue from being reflected in Atlantic waters!

Doune.

By sheer persistence, and employing an energetic hands-on style, Anderson proved a ferocious worker on behalf of the Callander & Oban. He managed to inspire construction of the line north-westwards from Callander, with only the hillside above Glen Ogle as its first destination. By sheer energy, and by hinting to his CR masters about possible NBR interference with a line into the Trossachs, Anderson succeeded in pushing the line on, through some of Scotland's most arresting scenery. The railway opened to Killin in 1870 (actually to a point some 200 feet above the village of that name), to Tyndrum in 1873 and to Dalmally four years later. The longer the line, the less sense it made for the Caledonian to walk away from it as they might have been tempted to do – revenue was limited in such sparsely-populated country.

Doune looking along the platform from the bridge.

Callander.

Callander.

Strathyre.

Finally, boosted by investment from the London & North Western Railway, far away at Euston, Anderson succeeded in raising funding for the final push – round Ben Cruachan and down through the Pass of Brander to the saltwater of Loch Etive. Oban was reached in 1880, the railway boxing the compass before entering from the south. An alarming proposal originally made to cross the bay to the North Pier on an embankment was quietly dropped.

The Caledonian found the line difficult to operate, and there can have been few railways where geology has been such a continuing factor in daily operation. Rock falls proved a problem in Glen Ogle from the start, while the geomorphology of Ben Cruachan includes a terrain of individual boulders just waiting to roll on to, or over, the railway and into Loch Awe below. 'Anderson's Piano' was the solution – a system of fences incorporating signal wires and directly controlling double-headed semaphores (unique in Britain then and now) which would warn drivers of a fall sufficient to breach the fence and damage the track below. The fences' nickname came from the sound of high wind in the wires. Even now, these signals – not unlike those seen in the Canadian Rockies – are still extant in the Pass of Brander.

Balquhidder.

Balquhidder Station, Balquhidder

The Caledonian built two classes of 'Bogie' locomotives to operate the line, the first of these being 4-4-0s designed by George Brittain in 1882. With their unprepossessing boilers and primitive cabs, they looked ill-suited for winter service on a line through such an environment, but they appear to have served the company well for the best of 30 years, although not all of it on the Oban line. Not long after the turn of the century, J.F. McIntosh introduced his '55' class of 4-6-0 for Callander & Oban service, and these operated on the line until the 1930s. They were succeeded by 'Clan' 4-6-0s transferred by the LMS from the former Highland Railway, before the arrival of the ubiquitous Stanier 'Black Five'. These became as common on the line as the two-coach DMU is now.

Killin Junction.

Loch Tay Pier.

One vehicle unique to this most fascinating of railways, was the Maid of Morven Pullman observation coach. Uniquely graced with a bow window at the rear, this took Scottish rail comfort into a new league, and was unequalled until BR introduced former LNER observation vehicles on to the West Highland in the 1950s (and the latter did not provide a Pullman service). How unfortunate it was that this vehicle was introduced on 3 August 1914, one day before the commencement of World War One and the Caledonian was never able to exploit the publicity value of this unique vehicle. It ran on the 8 am out of Glasgow (Buchanan Street), and the 3 pm return from Oban; a supplement of 2/6 was charged. More conventional Pullman cars were also rostered on Oban services after World War One – what a contrast to the utilitarian diesel of the present day!

Crianlarich.

Taynuilt, with the snow-capped bulk of Ben Cruachan above.

Rock falls have never been entirely eradicated from the story of the Callander & Oban. With BR considering transferring all Oban traffic to the West Highland line at Crianlarich – the two lines to the south had a spur connection here from 1894 – their hand was forced by nature. Closure notices for the Callander-Crianlarich section were already being circulated in September 1965 when a major rock fall in Glen Ogle created a blockage which would have taken a month to clear. As the section was due to close in five weeks anyway, no alternative to abandonment was possible, and the line closed immediately, with all traffic being rerouted up and down the West Highland line. The site of the rock fall is still visible to motorists on the A85, on the other side of the glen.

The Callander & Oban provided a trunk for a number of interesting branches. Killin was the first destination for the shrewd Anderson as he built the line stage by stage, but the station was four miles west of the village and some 200 feet higher. However, from March 1886 a line served the village, along with an extension to the shore of Loch Tay. Curiously, it had not required an Act of Parliament to build it, since no one had opposed. Although just over five miles long, the line was the product of a separate company, the Killin Railway Company maintaining its own existence until the Grouping of 1923. When that happened, the Company Secretary, seeing 'Euston' on correspondence, thought his company was being taken over by the London & North Western!

Connel Bridge under construction in 1901.

Oban.

The Killin Railway had a kenspeckle history. Its contractor underestimated building costs so severely that he went bankrupt, yet his use of concrete for the Dochart Viaduct greatly impressed the Board of Trade inspector. Two saddle-tanks provided by Dugald Drummond for the operation of the line proved unsuitable, and 0-4-4 tanks operated the line for many years. The Loch Tay extension provided connections with steamers on the loch, but this traffic ceased with the opening of the Second World War, and the little terminus there closed. Killin village continued to enjoy a passenger service until September 1965 – a BR 'Standard' 2-6-4 tank operated the line that summer on this author's only visit – but the branch was a victim of the Glen Ogle rock fall, since no connections to and from the south could be expected, except the long way round via Crianlarich and the West Highland.

Connel Bridge with Falls of Lora in flow.

Even more dramatic than the Killin Railway, was the Ballachulish Branch. This grew out of an ambitious Callander & Oban attempt to turn northwards from their destination of Oban, and penetrate farther up the West Coast and even up the Great Glen to Inverness. While the latter was never a serious option – with even the Caledonian formally opposing it, never mind the Highland and NBR as well – a line to the slate-producing village of Ballachulish was practical.

Two major viaducts had to be constructed before the branch could open in August 1903. One of these, the Connel Ferry Bridge over that part of saltwater Loch Etive known as the Falls of Lora, was to become one of Scotland's most impressive. A steel suspension bridge, it still has a modern appearance, tempered only by the traditional masonry approach spans. Nowadays, the line carries only single file road traffic since its closure to passenger trains in 1966, freight traffic having already been suspended in the previous year. Closure to rail produced an air of celebration in the district, the Callander & Oban having stolidly refused even pedestrian use of the bridge without a toll being paid. There could scarcely have been a quicker way of alienating local people against their railway.

Creagan Viaduct.

Kentallen.

Ballachulish.

Lochearnhead

St. Fillans.

Crieff.

Methven.

Almond Bank *.

* The village name is Almondbank, the station name was Almond Bank.

Locomotives 1894-1922

721, 4-4-0 built 1896, the *Dunalastair*.

In its final 25 years, the Caledonian was a 'big engine' line. It pioneered the 4-6-0 wheel classification for express work, introduced Pacific tank engines on its fast suburban services, and 0-8-0s for mineral traffic. No other Scottish company introduced such heavy units on to their networks; indeed, few companies anywhere in Britain could match this record. In particular the Great Western Railway and the LNWR copied the Caledonian in its building of 4-6-0s for express work, and that was a compliment indeed.

After Drummond's departure in 1890, his post was filled by Hugh Smellie, previously on the Maryport & Carlisle and Glasgow & South Western systems. Unfortunately, he died within a few months of taking office, and was succeeded by John Lambie. The latter continued Drummond's good work with a new 'edition' of 4-4-0s which included No. 17, the 'racer' which was to win the 1895 Race to Aberdeen for its makers. Lambie also contributed a class of 4-4-0 condensing tank engines for the low level service, and these were to have a long working life. More than their designer – Lambie died in office in 1895. His employers decided to promote internally, appointing their own John Farquharson McIntosh, Chief Inspector of the Running Department.

747, 0-6-0, built 1896.

780, 4-4-0 built 1898, last of the Dunalastair II to be built.

The Caledonian's fourth locomotive designer in little more than five years, McIntosh rapidly established his reputation with the introduction of a series of express 4-4-0 locomotives known as the 'Dunalastairs'. The fifteen examples of the 'Dunalastair I' class went into service in 1896, their name commemorating the Perthshire estate of one of the company directors. These were neat inside-cylinder engines which underwent successive refinements, each consolidating the reputation of the class. To the modern eye, the Drummond imprint can still be seen – the perfectly-balanced front end, the sandbox merged with the front splasher, and the cab still as lacking in creature comforts as anything designed by the autocratic Drummond.

These engines immediately began to work the company's Anglo-Scottish services with distinction, but McIntosh was not satisfied and produced the 'Dunalastair II' design in the following year. The main improvement was the lengthening of the smokebox, while the sanders were relocated below the running-plate, a change believed by many observers to be more aesthetically-satisfying, although that is a matter of opinion.

893, 4-4-0 built 1900, one of a class unofficially known as Dunalastair III.

784, 0-6-0T, built 1898.

600, 0-8-0, built 1901.

492, 0-8-0T, built 1903.

904, 4-6-0, built 1906.

More importantly, McIntosh introduced the double-bogie tender with a 5,000 gallon water capacity – a boon to hard-pressed crews trying to run the Carlisle-Stirling stretch, or even Carlisle-Glasgow, on a single tank of water. Railway historians must regret that the LMS did not copy McIntosh by supplying the 1938 'Coronation' Pacifics with a bogie tender of corresponding size; this Pacific Class failed to equal its LNER rival, the A4, for longevity of service. The A4 enjoyed the benefit of an eight-wheel 5,000 gallon tender, although not a double-bogie, like McIntosh's engines.

This second marque of the 'Dunalastair' brand inspired admiration at home and abroad, resulting in the Caledonian receiving an approach from the Belgian government for permission to copy the design. No fewer than 225 'copies' were produced, with the cab controls altered to right-hand drive, and some 0-6-0s were also built to McIntosh's design. The last of these, supposedly in preservation, was cut up as recently as the year 2002.

181, 4-6-0, built 1914.

185, 4-6-0, built 1914.

But McIntosh was not finished in refining the breed, producing the 'Dunalastair III' in 1899. There were only detail differences between these 16 engines, and the 'II' which preceded them, but there was no doubt about their ability. As observed in the chapter 'Racing Days', it was a 'III' numbered 899 which showed the East Coast companies a thing or two with its 108 minute dash from Carlisle to Edinburgh in the 1901 Race.

While this did not improve on No. 123's epic runs in the 1888 contest, we know that 899 was checked twice in the Beattock area, presumably by a preceding train not getting out of the way quickly enough. Even after the introduction of superheated versions of this 4-4-0 design, enginemen at Carlisle's Kingmoor depot believed they could reach Beattock faster with a saturated (unsuperheated) engine, the Caledonian's renowned historian A.G. Dunbar, recording that the older engines 'in the hands of an enterprising crew, could show strange bursts of speed at times'. Superheating involved returning newly-generated steam back through the boiler to be dried by gases from the fire and thus remove possible damage to the cylinders from undischarged water drops.

163, 0-4-4T, built 1915.

Hill-climbing and lower coal-consumption figures gave superheating the advantage in the long-term, however, and it was one of the 'IV' Class which became the first superheated engine in Scotland. This was No. 139, outshopped by St. Rollox in July 1910.

From this time on, the earlier 'IV's were converted to superheating, and nearly all future express engine construction would incorporate this improvement. Increased chimney diameter was usually the easiest way to identify a superheated engine on first sight, but the 'IV' still carried a disappointingly Spartan cab. The new 4-4-0s were rostered to the services between Carlisle and Perth, the most demanding on the Caledonian system, Dunbar describing them as 'probably the hardest worked engines of the type in Scotland'.

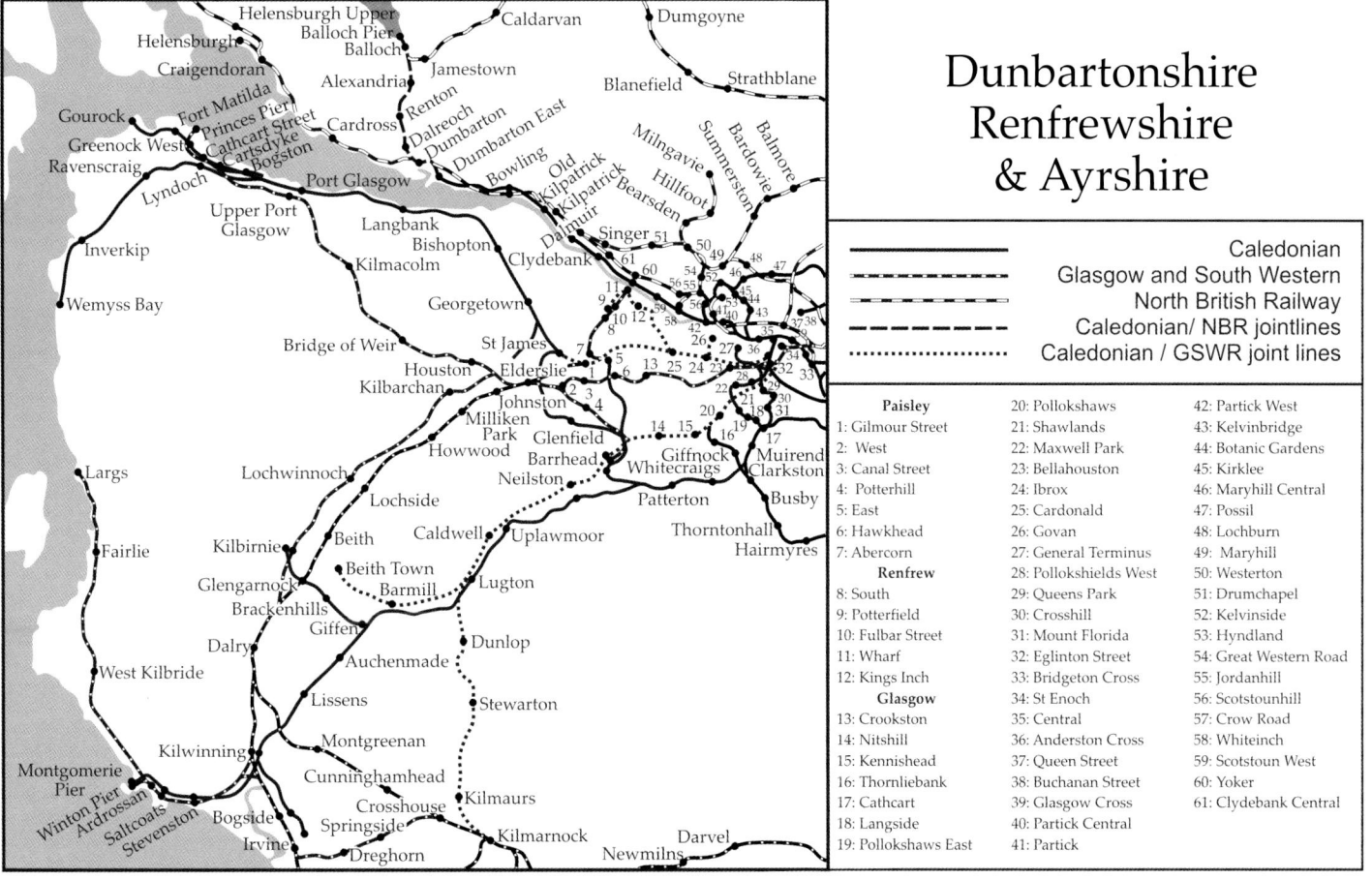

Clydebank.

Dunbartonshire Renfrewshire & Ayrshire

———	Caledonian
====	Glasgow and South Western
—•—•—	North British Railway
— — —	Caledonian/ NBR jointlines
········	Caledonian / GSWR joint lines

Paisley
1: Gilmour Street
2: West
3: Canal Street
4: Potterhill
5: East
6: Hawkhead
7: Abercorn

Renfrew
8: South
9: Potterfield
10: Fulbar Street
11: Wharf
12: Kings Inch

Glasgow
13: Crookston
14: Nitshill
15: Kennishead
16: Thornliebank
17: Cathcart
18: Langside
19: Pollokshaws East
20: Pollokshaws
21: Shawlands
22: Maxwell Park
23: Bellahouston
24: Ibrox
25: Cardonald
26: Govan
27: General Terminus
28: Pollokshields West
29: Queens Park
30: Crosshill
31: Mount Florida
32: Eglinton Street
33: Bridgeton Cross
34: St Enoch
35: Central
36: Anderston Cross
37: Queen Street
38: Buchanan Street
39: Glasgow Cross
40: Partick Central
41: Partick
42: Partick West
43: Kelvinbridge
44: Botanic Gardens
45: Kirklee
46: Maryhill Central
47: Possil
48: Lochburn
49: Maryhill
50: Westerton
51: Drumchapel
52: Kelvinside
53: Hyndland
54: Great Western Road
55: Jordanhill
56: Scotstounhill
57: Crow Road
58: Whiteinch
59: Scotstoun West
60: Yoker
61: Clydebank Central

Bowling.

After the Grouping in 1923, the new London Midland & Scottish company drafted its new compound 4-4-0s on to former Caledonian lines in Scotland, much to the disbelief of the GSWR's historian David L. Smith. He wrote that he and his enginemen colleagues couldn't believe that the new company would send compounds on to a system 'which had perfectly good 4-4-0s already!' It was an engineman's – a rival engineman's – tribute to the Caledonian's stud of 'Dunalastairs', and an example of the misplaced traction policy of the LMS (see chapter 'The End of the Caledonian Railway').

The 4-6-0 wheel arrangement was popular with locomotive designers all over the world in the age of steam power. British Railways was still building them into the late 1950s, giving the configuration a heritage in this country stretching back more than 60 years. The first British 4-6-0 was Scottish and was built by David Jones of the Highland Railway in 1894, for freight duties on that system. It was rapidly assumed in the railway industry that having a third pair of driving wheels on a bogie locomotive necessitated a longer, but narrower and more shallow, firebox. Express designs around this time favoured the 'Atlantic' 4-4-2 configuration, with an unpowered pair of wheels allowing a deeper firebox.

McIntosh saw no problem when he decided to consolidate the reputation he had forged for himself with the 'Dunalastairs' on the 'Caley'. Because he believed in designing high-pitched boilers as close to the maximum profile as the loading gauge would allow, there was no theoretical reason why he could not design a 4-6-0 design for the Caledonian and so, in 1902, that is what he did.

The first of no fewer than six different CR 4-6-0 Classes designed by McIntosh was a class of ten for the Callander & Oban line. The 55 Class were powerful machines, with their five-foot coupled wheels making them ideal for hill-climbing.

If the railway world was impressed by this new generation of 'Oban Bogie', it was nothing compared to the reception given to the next Caledonian 4-6-0 Class. Nos. 49 and 50, built in the following year, were designed for express work on the West Coast Main Line, having 78 inch driving wheels. Their boilers appeared enormous, but, coupled to an eight-wheel tender, these engines seemed in perfect proportion. By contrast, the LMS Royal Scot 4-6-0s of 1927, married a loco with a huge boiler to a 'Hornby'-like tender.

Balloch.

Georgetown, later known as Houston, built to serve the Royal Ordnance Factory.

With No. 50 named Sir James Thompson after the CR Chairman, the Caledonian now had a class of engines capable of taking 300 tons unassisted over Beattock, and this was a logical development of the 'Dunalastairs'. They reflected this lineage quite visibly, with their smokebox wingplates giving them a traditional appearance when seen head on. The designer's use of inside cylinders however, gave the engines a period air, and St.. Rollox would turn to the more modern outside cylinder as standard within 15 years.

Soon after 49 and 50, McIntosh produced a variation on the design, the six newer 4-6-0s being headed by No. 903 Cardean. This particular engine was soon allocated to hauling the 2pm up 'Corridor' express (later known as the 'Midday Scot'), and its corresponding northbound working back from Carlisle to Glasgow. Cardean and her sisters were capable of high power outputs when tested against locomotives on other lines, and they also established a reputation for reliability, No. 903 coming to be identified with the 'Corridor' as her regular roster.

Langbank.

It is noticeable to the historian that when high-speed turns were accomplished on the Caledonian, it was the 'Dunalastairs' which were making the sparks fly. In his book *Main Lines Across the Border*, O.S. Nock conceded that No. 903 rarely reached Beattock punctually on the down 2pm, but could regain time when climbing the bank itself. McIntosh's 4-6-0s were shire horses; the 4-4-0s were the greyhounds.

An initial problem with the 4-6-0s was their length. They were too long for the turntable at Kingmoor Depot, the Carlisle fitters becoming adept at separating engine from tender to allow them to be turned separately, and then reuniting them, all within 20 minutes. At the Glasgow end, the Cathcart circle was used to turn the engines, all this going on until 70 feet turntables were installed in 1906.

McIntosh built three more classes of 4-6-0, although not for the company's premier services. These were the '908' Class, for Clyde Coast trains, and the '918', whose 60 inch driving wheels made them ideal for fast freight services, both outshopped in 1906. A later variation on the '908' was the '179' Class, also with 69 inch driving wheels, constructed in 1913-15.

Port Glasgow.

Greenock Central.

Goods traffic was also served by the '812' Class of 0-6-0s, augmenting the stud of 'Jumbo's begun by Drummond. There were no fewer than 96 of the McIntosh variety – and one is preserved today, more than any of his 4-4-0s, unfortunately.

With mineral traffic bringing in a 50% increase in revenue in the 1890s, an even bigger locomotive to service this kind of traffic was required, and McIntosh responded with two 0-8-0 designs. Eight tender versions of these were built from 1901, with six examples of a tank version also being constructed. The former were rated as the most powerful engines in Scotland, but they proved difficult to maintain, and it was noticeable that the NBR, with an equally demanding mineral traffic to service, contented itself with the 0-6-0. The 'Caley' certainly had no complaints about theirs, nearly all the examples of the latter wheel arrangement going back to Drummond's time, finding useful employment well into British Railways' days.

Greenock West.

Fort Matilda.

McIntosh was never frightened to experiment, producing five examples of a 'Mogul' 2-6-0 design (Scotland's first) but obviously a 'stretched' version' of an 0-6-0, and none too successful. However, more interesting were his designs for both 'Atlantic' and 'Pacific' express locomotive types. These never saw the light of day, but are described in some detail in Mr Nock's book on the Caledonian. Like him, we can only regret that prototypes were not proceeded with – in particular, the sight of a McIntosh 'Pacific' with outside-cylinders (four in all) would have been fascinating.

Gourock.

Greenock Upper.

Wemyss Bay.

'Wemyss Bay' Tank, No. 953.

Ardrossan, Montgomerie Pier.

Montgomerie Pier.

McIntosh retired in 1914, the year when Britain was plunged into World War One. His successor was William Pickersgill, who had held a similar, although obviously less demanding, post, with the Great North of Scotland Railway. Historians have been less than kind to Pickersgill; not long after his appointment he made the mistake of trying to improve on the 'Dunalastair' breed. Although an expert on superheating, the new Locomotive Superintendent failed to produce any marked improvement in the design (which would have been difficult), although the 48 4-4-0s which he built were long-lasting, all of them passing through Grouping in 1923 and Nationalisation in 1948, with some examples operating into the early 1960s.

He seems to have had less success with his 4-6-0 designs. He built three classes 'none of which can be said to have been very good', according to locomotive historian Campbell Highet. The first of these were the Class '60' 'Greybacks' of 1916-17, which were good enough for the LMS to add 20 more to the six the Caledonian produced, and Highet concedes that one of them acquitted itself well on test. A number of the LMS-built examples passed into British Railways ownership, some being allocated to the 'lions' den' of St. Margaret's, the former NBR loco headquarters in Edinburgh.

Saltcoats.

By the time the '60's had appeared – the first 'home-made' class of main line engines to have outside cylinders since 1882 – the company had taken over six locomotive 'orphans'. These were the River Class built for the Highland Railway in 1915 by Frederic Godfrey Smith, but which proved unacceptable to the line's civil engineer. Handsome machines though they were, they precipitated Smith's resignation, while his employers cheerfully sold the engines on to the Caledonian – when Scapa Flow traffic was at its heaviest through the Highland Railway system – and for more than the Highland had paid for them! It was a good bargain for the 'Caley' too, and their arrival confirmed the trend towards outside cylinders on the company's express engines.

Pickersgill's other 4-6-0s comprised the '956' and '191' Classes, neither of which distinguished themselves in locomotive lore. The former were constructed with three cylinders, conjugated valve gear being worked off the middle cylinder between the frames. It was not a successful experiment, and even the great Sir Nigel Gresley had trouble with the arrangement in years to come. The '191' Class, intended for the Oban line, had problems of its own. For no apparent good reason, the class was built unsuperheated, some 12 years after a 'Dunalastair IV' had demonstrated the advantages of superheating. Not surprisingly, Campbell Highet described them as 'somewhat unsatisfactory in service'.

Irvine.

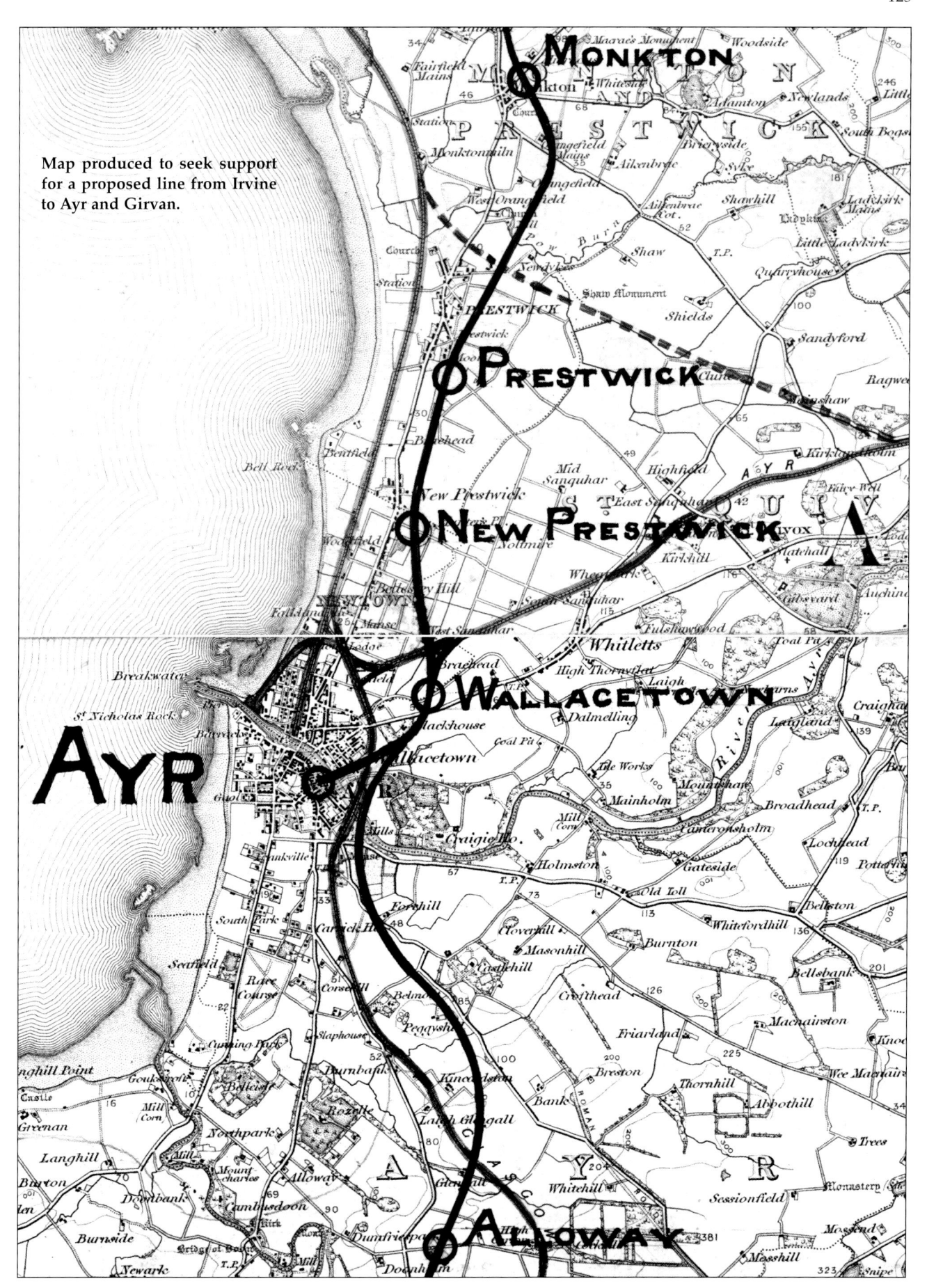

Map produced to seek support for a proposed line from Irvine to Ayr and Girvan.

Stewarton

More successful were Pickersgill's 'Wemyss Bay' tanks. These were unique in Scotland in having a 'Pacific', 4-6-2, configuration, and were designed to operate fast suburban services on the Clyde Coast. They were not unknown on Edinburgh-Glasgow express work, and undertook banking duties at Beattock from quite early on in their careers. Introduced in 1917, six were still operating as the 1950s dawned.

If the Caledonian earned its description as a 'big engine' line, this certainly didn't apply at one point in the Tay Valley. At Inchture, a 1-mile branch went off to the village of that name, the 1910 timetable showing six return trips daily. Nothing remarkable about that, but what was unusual about the service was that it was literally horse-powered until the closure of the branch in 1917.

This made it unique in Scotland, although the NBR had once tried to fob off both South Leith and North Berwick with such a service, before deciding to relegate their stagecoach-like 'Dandy' vehicle to service the transport needs of the unfortunate English citizens of Port Carlisle. Judging from illustrations, Inchture travellers were luckier, the 'Caley' vehicle being quite an attractive tram, boasting the Scottish coat of arms on its side. The 'Caley' did nothing by halves, even when doing things by half!

Dunlop.

Uplawmoor.

Inchture.

Racing Days

Luncarty.

With so much duplication built into the 19th century British railway network, it's perhaps surprising that there were not more examples of racing between companies serving the same destination. History shows us that, with the exception of some competition among English companies to bring transatlantic passengers and mails from southern ports up to London, Britain's only racetracks were the East and West Coast lines, between London, Edinburgh, and Aberdeen.

Racing took place in three separate summer seasons – 1888, 1895, and 1901. Readers wishing to learn more about this extraordinary sequence of competitive railroading, particularly in the first two years mentioned, can do no better than read O.S. Nock's *Railway Race to the North* (unfortunately out of print at the time of writing, although well worth searching for in libraries or secondhand bookshops).

Strathord.

The Caledonian was outstanding in all three of these outbursts of racing. Locomotives of three different classes were used, men from at least three depots – it mattered not who or what was involved, the 'Caley' got on with it. The job was done with an élan which gratified the company's southern partner, the London & North Western, and disconcerted its East Coast rivals, both north and south.

Pressure for improvements in daytime Anglo-Scottish services in 1888 seems to have emanated entirely from the English companies, beginning with the Midland's decision to abandon the Second Class category of travel, and admit Third Class passengers to all its trains. The East Coast replied by opening up their services to all classes on all trains except the 10 am out of King's Cross, and this, the forerunner of the 'Flying Scotsman', rapidly assumed an eminence which began to outshine its ten o'clock counterpart out of Euston.

Coupar Angus.

Alyth Junction.

A number of accelerations were introduced as the summer days lengthened in 1888, but almost entirely at the expense of the digestion of passengers. In those days before restaurant cars, lunches were taken at Preston on the West Coast, York on the East (and Normanton on the Midland), with the meal interval being whittled down to 20 minutes. This was for the consumption of four courses, plus coffee!

By the end of July, the railway staffs were having to make their own contribution to timesaving, not an easy task on the LNWR, where speed was looked on as an expensive commodity in terms of timekeeping and maintenance. But some response became necessary when the East Coast announced that their ten o'clock service would reach Edinburgh in 8 hours. The two West Coast allies agreed to match this on 1 August, but realised that they had a fight on their hands when the East Coast train entered Waverley (the rival trains terminated at opposite ends of Edinburgh's Princes Street) on that day in eight hours flat.

Isla Valley.

Auldbar Road.

Dubton Junction.

Preparations were now made for a West Coast reply on the following Monday – unfortunately, a Bank Holiday, with all the extra traffic that that would generate. The 'Caley' agreed to take the racer forward from Carlisle to Edinburgh in 112 minutes, a challenging timing for a 100-mile route which included not only the ten miles of Beattock Bank, but a second gradient of almost equal severity up to the 880 feet high summit at Cobbinshaw, begun straight off a speed-restricted curve between Strawfrank and Dolphinton Junctions (effectively, where the Edinburgh line left the Glasgow route, and joined the lines from Carstairs Station).

For this challenge, the Caledonian eschewed the use of its latest fleet of 4-4-0s, and introduced No. 123 to the world. This was a single-wheeler, a 4-2-2 of elegant design, delivered by Glasgow's Neilson company, although Drummond's specification was almost certainly followed by the builders. This fine machine can still be viewed at Glasgow's Museum of Transport.

112 minutes to Edinburgh? No problem for No. 123, which reeled off the distance with eight minutes to spare! And this was just the beginning, with a later journey, on 9 August, being run in 102 minutes. Nor was this untypical. Mr Nock records that the train averaged less than 108 minutes for all journeys throughout the month of August 1888, at an average speed of 56 mph. He points out that "to this engine fell the task of securing the early arrivals of the West Coast train … at Carlisle the train could not be started earlier". This was for timetable reasons, as the crew waited for 'time', but that inhibition went out the window in both 1895 and 1901.

Laurencekirk.

Fordoun.

Drumlithie summit.

Stonehaven.

Not only was the single achieving impressive average speeds, she was expected to, with a timetabled average higher than the LNWR had set itself south of Crewe. Indeed, nothing on the East Coast equalled this challenge on paper, apart from the York-Newcastle timing, which the NER had some difficulty in meeting anyway. And nowhere on either line, east or west, was there an incline to be climbed as long and as hard as Beattock or Cobbinshaw! The work of No. 123 was unequalled in the 1888 Race to the North.

1895 saw a different type of race. Following the opening of the Forth Bridge and the doubling of approaches east and west of Waverley Station, the East Coast companies were now in a position to improve their timetabled services to Aberdeen, a destination which previously the Caledonian had regarded as its own. This time overnight services were involved, with both East and West Coast companies running an 8pm out of King's Cross and Euston respectively. A fifth partner was involved, with the NBR coming in north of Edinburgh, but more importantly, there was to be a 'winning post'.

Stonehaven – Aberdeen local

Muchalls.

While the racers of 1888 terminated about a mile apart in Edinburgh, much to the inconvenience of enthusiasts and journalists following the conflict with unabated interest, seven years later, the racing trains were heading for Kinnaber Junction. Here, approximately 38 miles south of Aberdeen, the NBR route joined the Caledonian line, exercising running-powers from there on to the Granite City. While one author has described the NBR as being 'beholden' to the Caledonian for this privilege, part of the West Coast route through the Monklands, north-east of Glasgow, required the Caledonian to hold running powers over a quarter-mile of NBR metals. A ransom strip indeed.

On paper, the East Coast had the shorter route to Kinnaber – by some 17 miles over the Forth and Tay bridges. But this advantage was purely nominal when the poorly-engineered character of the NBR route through Fife and Angus is considered, and there are few main lines in the UK more difficult to operate. On the other hand, the Caledonian line was designed as an express route, and this was as true north of the Forth-Clyde isthmus as south of it. In particular the route through Strathmore, north from Perth, was perfect for racing. The Caledonian must have approached the idea of a Race to Aberdeen with quiet confidence.

Portlethen.

135

Aberdeen.

From Perth to Aberdeen

Caledonian Railway
North British Railway
Highland Railway
Great North of Scotland Railway
Caledonian/ NBR joint lines

1: Magdalen Green
2: Esplanade
3: Dundee West
4: Tay Bridge
5: Dundee East
6: Stannergate
7: West Ferry
8: Maryfield
9: Lochee
10: Lochee West
11: West Newport
12: East Newport
13: Tayport

Bankfoot.

In his definitive book, Mr Nock is careful not to name the winner of the 1895 contest, but it has to be the West Coast consortium, if only for their determination to race night after night until their rivals cried 'Enough'. Which is exactly what the East Coast did after their overnight run on 21 and 22 August, a journey which ended in an impressive victory for a NBR Holmes 4-4-0 crossing the Kinnaber 'finishing line' first.

However, after accounting for themselves so well, the East Coast companies, like the highly-efficient German High Seas fleet at the Battle of Jutland in 1916, left the battlefield to a bloodied but defiant victor. On the next night, the Caledonian staff played their part in an emphatic performance, reaching Aberdeen in 8 hours 32 minutes, an average speed in excess of 63 mph over more than 500 miles.

Alyth Junction.

Newtyle, old station.

The Caledonian's part in the 1895 clash consisted of running the 203 miles from Carlisle to Kinnaber at an average of more than 60 mph, usually with a stop at Stirling as well as Perth. Although the line was well-engineered, particularly compared to the NBR's Edinburgh-Aberdeen switchback, there were still a number of problems which had to be overcome by the two crews involved. Obviously, Beattock had to be climbed, as seven years previously, and, while the line north of there contained no summit as challenging as Cobbinshaw on the Edinburgh route, there was the constant problem of water supply.

Newtyle, new station.

Auchterhouse.

The LNWR had pioneered water troughs – a simple system of supply allowing a locomotive to scoop up water as it travelled over a set of shallow troughs set between the rails – but north of the Border, its partner company had none. In fact no Scottish company fitted troughs; the LMS put two sets on to the West Coast line north of Carlisle in the 1920s, at Mossband, near Gretna, and just south of Carstairs.

To run from Carlisle to Stirling without refreshing the tender's water supply was a challenge demanding the greatest economy of working – at a time when management were tearing the timetables to shreds and urging the crews to run as hard as they could! To put it in perspective, a Gresley Pacific, with 5,000 gallons 'in the tank' could cover the Newcastle-Edinburgh stretch of East Coast Main Line (124 miles) without a problem, but the 'Caley' run, from Carlisle to Stirling, was longer, and the tender capacity available to fill the boiler was some 1,500 gallons less.

Baldovan.

Yet, not once did 'Caley' enginemen have to make an unscheduled stop for water. In contrast, during the 1901 Race, a Midland crew found they had to stop their train to refill during their run through the Pennines. As a result, their NBR colleagues brought the train to its destination no less than 16 minutes behind its rival. A racing train stopping for water could whistle goodbye to victory.

Three locomotives carried the baton for the Caledonian in 1895. Taking over from the LNWR at Carlisle were one of two locomotives and crews. Archibald Crooks (known affectionately as 'Baldie') drove No. 90 on to Perth, sharing this duty on alternate nights with driver Tom Robinson at the regulator of No. 78. North of Perth, John Soutar was in charge of No. 17. All were 4-4-0s of Drummond design, although No. 17 had been turned out by his successor, John Lambie.

Lochee West.

Dundee Terminus, Dundee and Newtyle.

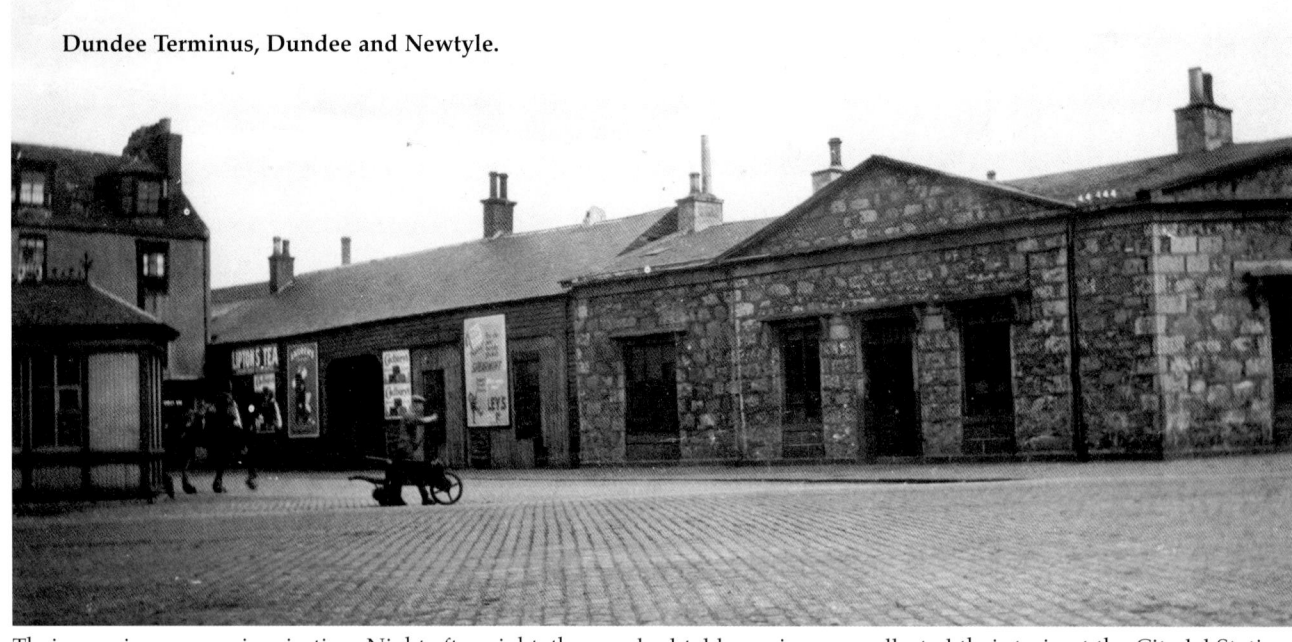

Their running was an inspiration. Night after night, these redoubtable enginemen collected their train at the Citadel Station, their explosive departure for the north thrilling the enthusiastic crowd – this at twenty to two in the morning! The well laid-out permanent way undoubtedly gave the crews the confidence to run at maximum speed, and no faint heart need dare question the wisdom of such a mode of travel. One passenger who did, losing his nerve and pulling the communication cord on the tearaway descent from Gleneagles to Perth, found that the cord was unconnected, its entire length piling up on the floor at his feet! On complaining to the ticket collector at Perth, he was emphatically told that, had he succeeded in stopping the train, he would have been fined! Presumably the Board of Trade failed to hear of this incident!

There is no space here for a full account of this episode of British railroading where trains raced from almost one end of the island to the other. A brief description of the Caledonian's contribution to the excitement on the morning of the 23 August, will have to suffice.

Dundee West.

Magdalen Green.

It began with 'Baldie' Crooks heading No. 90 out of Carlisle at 1.43 am, planning to run non-stop over the 150 miles to Stirling. He accomplished this at an average of just over 60 mph, Beattock included, with the engine being driven less than all-out in the early stages. Even after passing Stirling, No. 90 was still being driven circumspectly, and Mr Nock concludes in his definitive work on the 1888 and 1895 Races, that some three minutes were lost on the approach to Perth while 'Baldie' ensured that the water would last. Running low on water to feed the boiler on route could lead to the top heating surface of the firebox being left dry, melting a unit known as a fusible plug and feeding the remaining water on to the fire. This was a disciplinary offence.

The run concluded with John Soutar burning up the track to Kinnaber, nearly 52 miles away, in 47 minutes, passing the junction at over 70 mph. There was no North British train in sight; the East Coast rivals were standing on their dignity. Meanwhile, Soutar was going through Stonehaven at 80! The racer, the last of those of 1895 vintage, was into Aberdeen at 4.32 am, where, needless to say, a crowd awaited. Soutar and his fireman were borne shoulder-high through the cheering throng, and the company later published a log of the run, and a picture postcard featuring Soutar.

The run did not end happily for everyone. A transport journalist who demanded milk for his porridge at the station hotel, was told 'The coos are no milkit yet!' And there we must leave the Caledonian's contribution to the Race of 1895.

Invergowrie.

Inchture.

The Race of 1901 was less well-documented than the previous two, and had its origins in circumstances which did not involve the Caledonian at all. Its Scottish rival, the North British, received Anglo-Scottish traffic over two different routes, from the Berwick direction from the North Eastern Railway, and from the Midland at Carlisle. The Edinburgh company's relations with the NER were not good, the latter company operating Anglo-Scottish express into the heart of Edinburgh through generously-granted running-powers. Meanwhile the Midland, a heavy investor in services to Scotland (and in the Forth Bridge consortium) could never lose sight of the fact that the NBR was working with companies the Midland regarded as deadly rivals.

Suffice to say that, when the Midland and NBR accelerated their 9.30 am from St. Pancras to Edinburgh, the North Eastern immediately started to bring the northbound 'Flying Scotsman' into Edinburgh as early as NBR signalmen would permit them, with no reference to the agreed timetable, or to the 1896 timing agreement (of which more later). When the newspapers picked up on this, they immediately dubbed it a Race and began to report Edinburgh arrival times, at both Waverley, but also at Princes Street. In other words, the Caledonian found itself 'competing' in what should have been a domestic disagreement between two East Coast companies!

Show a bull a red rag, and the result is predictable. On 5 July 1901, after four days of the North Eastern showing the North British a clean pair of heels, the 10 am out of Euston rolled into Princes Street Station, 35 minutes early. The porters were having their afternoon cup of tea at the time! Dunalastair III 4-4-0 No. 899 had run the 100 miles from Carlisle, over Beattock and Cobbinshaw Summits, in 108 minutes, and arrived some 29 minutes ahead of the East Coast arrival at the other end of the street. No better than No. 123 you might think, but 899 had been affected by two signal checks in the Beattock area, probably caused by a preceding train failing to take refuge in the Summit loops in sufficient time.

Kirriemuir.

It was a brilliant achievement in the circumstances, but was unacknowledged in the specialist railway press of the time. The North Eastern certainly acknowledged it, bringing an overnight train into Waverley in four minutes less the next morning. But the 'Caley' was back on top by the evening, eight minutes ahead of the NER. To be fair, the latter was almost certainly receiving obstructive treatment, on the last stage of the journey, from NBR signalmen north of Berwick.

The weekend then intervened, with the Scottish holiday season in full swing whereas in contrast, the other two racing periods took place during the English holiday month of August. On 8 July, the Midland and North British made a mighty effort, pipping the North Eastern at Portobello East Junction (the 'Kinnaber' of 1901) by four minutes. The Caledonian was only two minutes behind, demonstrating again that, if you wanted a race, the 'Caley' would give you one, any time. The 1901 Race then fizzled out, with the North British summoning enough diplomacy to placate its two warring allies. More information on this, the least well-known of the three races, can be found in this author's *The Railway Race to Scotland 1901*. The three races of 1888, 1895, and 1901 brought nothing but credit to the Caledonian Railway at the time, but they had a disastrous effect on Anglo-Scottish express services in the long term. On the credit side, the Caledonian had shown that it was fit to take its place in the top echelon of British railway companies. A worthy partner to the LNWR – described by some journalists as the 'Premier Line' – it was a feared opponent for any company contesting its reputation for speed, as the NBR discovered. While the East Coast companies had successfully braced themselves to make an impressive one-off challenge, the 'Caley' had demonstrated, apparently effortlessly, that it could run at maximum express speeds, day and night, week after week – as a matter of course. This, after all, was what the Caledonian was designed to be – nothing less than an 'expressway' into, and throughout, Scotland. On the debit side, the 1896 agreement, with its upper limit of 8 hours between London and Edinburgh and Glasgow, was made between East and West Coast concerns to reassure the public on the question of safety. However, it became more binding as the years went on, resulting in the LMS in the early 1930s being constrained to operate its new 'Royal Scot' locomotives, and the LNER its Gresley Pacifics, to the same timings that 4-4-0 locomotives had attained with ease in the 1890s! Worse, the LMS was actually building more 4-4-0s in the 1930s.

Friockheim.

Arbroath.

This deliberate slowing of express trains was a cartel against the public interest. Unfortunately, the media, less analytical than nowadays, failed to question why no accelerations seemed possible on such trains as the 'Royal Scot'. Not surprisingly, rival modes of transport started up between London and Scotland, particularly bus services, although in 1928 it was noticeable that the operators could not guarantee any time of arrival! Journey time by bus between Glasgow and London by the early 1930s could be reasonably predicted by the operators as 16 hours by then, but one motoring agency in Buchanan Street was offering to drive seven passengers in a single day to London – by private car.

As late as the 1930s, when the Caledonian and LMS had been offering London-Edinburgh passenger services for over 80 years, travellers were still taking sea voyages between these cities. The rail companies (including the East Coast concerns) just couldn't kill off this passenger trade. And all because the rail companies imperiously believed that the public would accept their 'take it or leave it' attitude of imposing lax timetabling and fares far higher than those offered by rivals old and new.

Arbroath at street level.

Brechin.

Although there were accelerations from 1932, a direct answer to this snail's pace of transport came not just from road and sea, but also from above. When Anglo-Scottish air services began in 1934, eight of the first 70 flights failed to reach their destination. This is not as alarming as it might sound; weather conditions forced their curtailment at an airport en route. But the railways' monopolistic attitude had encouraged the emergence of this form of transport, even when it was not technically advanced enough to offer a reliable service.

In the light of all this, the LNER and LMS insistence on continuing the 1896 agreement up to 1932 – deliberately keeping Anglo-Scottish expresses down to a 48 mph average speed – was commercial madness. Even racing made more sense than that!

Edzell.

Caledonian Railway Stations – II

Bridge Street Station south of the Clyde in Glasgow, and Buchanan Street Station north of the river, were never going to be sufficient for a company as ambitious as the Caledonian. A major station on the north bank, but taking London and south Glasgow suburban traffic, was a priority for the company. There seems to have been no conception of the need for a through main line station, which could also have incorporated at least one terminal section.

As a result, London-Aberdeen expresses would avoid Glasgow (except in a few occasional cases) by travelling off the West Coast Main Line and through the Monklands to Castlecary and then northwards. On the East Coast Main Line Waverley was both a through station for London-Aberdeen and London-Perth services and also contained two termini configured back-to-back. Even in Edinburgh, the Caledonian thought in terminal terms, its Princes Street Station being a 'dead end' for long-distance traffic.

While the theory of a central Glasgow terminus may have been questionable, there was no doubt about the execution. With the GSWR newly installed at St. Enoch in 1876, pressure mounted on the Caledonian to establish a north bank terminus. The rival company's crossing of the Clyde finally removed those obstacles preventing the Caledonian from so doing, and the Admiralty's objections were met with a bridge into Gordon Street, although its width was restricted to 55 feet, only enough for four tracks.

Even as it opened in 1879, it became obvious that the new Central Station, with the London and Edinburgh traffic transferred to it immediately after opening, was inadequate. 173 trains daily transported nearly 5 million passengers annually from the start, and within 15 years these figures had nearly trebled, not including those for the new low level station, opened in 1896.

Central Station Glasgow.

GORDON STREET AND CENTRAL STATION, GLASGOW.

Central Station Glasgow.

CENTRAL STATION, GLASGOW.

In 1899 permission was obtained to substantially enlarge Central, along with the construction of a major new bridge over the Clyde. The new layout included main line platforms reaching up to the river's edge, while platforms 12 and 13 were wide enough to incorporate a cab rank. Signalling control was concentrated on a single two-storey box between the old and new bridges. Staffed by ten men, it did the work of three boxes and 22 men on a layout three times the extent of the previous area under their control. This semaphore system lasted until 1961 when replaced by colour-lights.

Typically, in the midst of all this upheaval, in 1903 the Caledonian sent engineer Donald Matheson on a study tour of the USA to ensure that the best international perspective could be acquired on contemporary station architecture.

The opening of Central in 1906 produced the biggest station in the UK at that time and also one of the finest buildings in Glasgow. Within a year of completion, passenger figures handled reached the 20 million mark. An established feature for them, and subsequent generations of travellers, is the one-storey 'Train Information' building overlooking the concourse, incorporating a serviced destination board. This was a city landmark, the public seemingly reassured that their trains might actually leave on time, and from the platform indicated, because it was obvious that there were real people behind the displays.

Princes Street Station, Edinburgh.

Edinburgh still awaited a terminus worthy of the city when the 1890s began, and it was not until 1893 that the new Princes Street Station was completed. Its profile was to change within ten years when the Caledonian Hotel opened above, the traveller being presented with the choice of two portals when approaching from Princes Street. The left-hand portal led (and still leads) into the hotel; the right-hand one opened into a concourse covered by a steel-framed glass roof 1,000 foot wide at one point. There were seven platforms, none of which had release loops, rendering essential the presence of a station pilot. Semaphore signalling was in use to the end of the station's life, which came in September 1965, when a new connection between former NBR and CR systems west of Haymarket allowed the transfer of services to Birmingham and Glasgow (Central) to Waverley. Suburban services to Balerno, Barnton, and Leith (North) had ended in 1943, 1951, and 1962 respectively.

Curiously, Princes Street Station had been rated by the City Valuation Officer in 1923 at £950, precisely half that of the Waverley. Somehow this seems to sum up the Caledonian's half-hearted approach to Edinburgh, a territory it seemed prepared to cede to its rival, the NBR, while regarding Glasgow jealously as it own.

Princes Street Station, Edinburgh.

Accidents and Incidents

Larbert, 29 April 1867.

The top of a red sandstone cross of Celtic design, glimpsed over a high graveyard wall, is the only indication to the passer-by in Edinburgh of a major reminder of Caledonian, and indeed, Scottish history. For Roseburn Cemetery, on the boundary between Edinburgh and Leith, is the poignant burial-place for no fewer than 214 members of the same regimental battalion. These Royal Scots were killed in 1915, not at the battles of Gallipoli or Loos which took place in that year, but in a Caledonian Railway accident near Gretna Green.

Coupar Angus, 20 August 1899.

Kirtlebridge, 6 April 1906.

Kirtlebridge, 6 April 1906.

Thankerton, 6 February 1908.

Thankerton, 6 February 1908.

AFTER THE ACCIDENT Nr CRAWFORD APRIL 2ND 1909 A.B.

The transport corridor north from Gretna through the valleys of the Annan and Evan Water, before crossing the Beattock watershed into Clydesdale, is one of the busiest in Scotland. The Caledonian began to build through this corridor in 1846 – resisting a temptation to transfer to the more populous Nithsdale route – and in the 1990s the motorway was extended northwards from Carlisle, with more environmental damage than the railway caused, it has to be said. This corridor is also the route followed from 30,000 feet above by air traffic between London and Edinburgh and Glasgow, as well as the last sight of land before transatlantic flights turn west to head for the New World.

Inevitably, it has seen its share of accidents. The A74 road was notorious for its poor safety record, and the Caledonian suffered two accidents before 1900 on this line, at Kirtlebridge and Lockerbie. The former happened in 1872 when the yard layout proved to be insufficiently interlocked to prevent an oncoming train colliding with a shunting movement. Eleven passengers and one railwayman died.

At Lockerbie in 1883, an accident happened because the company had been persuaded by its southern partner, the LNWR, to adopt the chain brake on Anglo-Scottish trains, despite its being technically inferior to the Caledonian's own choice of the Westinghouse system. Fortunately this was less serious than the Kirtlebridge incident, but had the long-term benefit of causing the Caledonian to put its foot down, as it were, and persist with its own choice of brake power.

Lockerbie too was the location of one of the world's worst aeronautical accidents, when a time-bombed Pan Am 747 exploded over the town in December 1988, killing 259 people on board and eleven unfortunates in the town below. This exceeded the death-toll at Quintinshill, but the accident there in May 1915 is still the worst in British railway history. Books such as L.T.C. Rolt's *Red for Danger* tell of this horrific accident in detail, so this account will be no more than a summary. Quintinshill is the location of the last signal box in Scotland north of the junction at Gretna, where the line from Carstairs southwards is joined by the former GSWR line from Glasgow and Dumfries. Nowadays, Quintinshill is an anonymous passing-place, but in 1915 this was a busy site, with relief loops on both up and down sides.

At the centre of the Quintinshill disaster was an early morning local train working northwards from Carlisle. On 22 May, the northbound express, which usually preceded the local, was running late, so the slow train was allowed to leave Carlisle first, before being stopped at Quintinshill to allow the express to overtake. Unfortunately, so heavy was wartime traffic that both the up and down loops were already occupied, so Signalman Meakin decided to shunt the local from the down (northbound) line to the up (southbound) to give a clear path for the express. This shunt completed, the train's fireman, Huchinson, came into the box to formally announce that his train was now stopped in the section, as the rules required him to do, but Meakin failed to put a collar on the signal levers protecting the now-occupied southbound track. This would have been a safeguard making it impossible to admit a southbound train into the section – and there was a train due. Meakin had already been warned that a troop special was heading for Liverpool and was making good time.

Meakin was at the end of his overnight shift and was due to be relieved by Signalman Tinsley, arriving from Gretna on the very local train which was now shunted on to the up track. Tinsley was arriving late, but there was an informal arrangement between him and Meakin that the latter would note entries in pencil for the log-book, allowing Tinsley to confirm the entries in ink. This was highly irregular, and Tinsley was occupied catching up with his paperwork in the first few minutes after his belated arrival. He also failed to attach the safety collars to the levers. Hutchinson failed to comment on this omission. When the box immediately to the north offered the speeding troop train, Tinsley unhesitatingly accepted it – with the local train blocking the track just a few yards away from him. Meanwhile, Meakin had retired to the back of the box where he had begun reading the morning newspaper Tinsley had brought him. He only looked up when he heard the thunder of an approaching train …

The subsequent carnage began with the collision between the speeding troop train, with its Dardanelles-bound Royal Scots, and the stationary local train. The devastation was aggravated by the use of antiquated wooden coaching-stock, lit by gas, in the train from the north, the wreckage of which now caught fire. But the signals were still set for the northbound express from Carlisle, and despite a desperate attempt to put these at danger, and even to flag down the express from the line side, this now ploughed into the debris.

Beith Town, 1909.

Beith Town, 11 July 1911.

Gretna Green (Quintinshill), 22 May 1915.

Burning train, Gretna Green Railway Disaster May 22, 1915.

Gretna Green (Quintinshill), 22 May 1915, wounded dressing station

227 people were killed in this terrible incident. Both signalmen were arrested and stood trial, along with Hutchinson, the fireman of the local train. The last-named was acquitted, although both Meakin and Tinsley were found guilty and imprisoned, the latter enduring three years of penal servitude.

One wonders if the company's management should also have been in the dock. No less than 43 years earlier, an invention called Track Circuiting was first tried out successfully in the USA. It was experimented with at King's Cross terminus in London, but not applied nationwide. It is difficult to see why not as all that was required was a small electrical charge, usually no more than 100 volts, to be fed along the rail itself, within signalling sections. Any train entering the section automatically short-circuited the current, illuminating a control panel light in the nearby box. It was a simple concept, cheap to run, and above all, was 'fail safe'. Any breakdown in the system indicated a broken circuit and therefore an occupied section, either automatically setting signals at danger, or at least giving an emergency signal to the signalman. If it was lax of the Caledonian Railway, and all other British companies, not to have installed track circuiting by 1915, it was infinitely worse that they failed to install it after Quintinshill.

Funeral of 100 victims of the Gretna Green disaster in Leith.

Alloa Swing Bridge. On the afternoon of 12 October 1904, a tug with a vessel in tow was passing underneath the bridge when it ran against one of the piers, bringing the pier and a section of the girder spans into the river.

Alloa Swing Bridge. In the early hours of 15 August 1920 an even more dramatic incident occurred. A surrendered German destroyer broke free from her mooring at South Alloa and travelled upstream on the flow tide. Striking the bridge roughly midway between the swing section and the Throsk end, she completely destroyed one of the stone piers and brought two of the girder spans down.

While understandably concentrating on the carelessness and lack of professionalism of Meakin and Tinsley, the reporting accident inspector, Colonel Druitt, felt that there was no need for track circuiting at Quintinshill, in view of the simplicity of the layout there, with unrestricted views to north and south. This was an extraordinary let-off for the Caledonian in more ways than one. Druitt seemed to forget that half of a railway's work is undertaken in darkness, and that fog and mist are not exactly unknown in Dumfriesshire, as elsewhere. Not only that, but the view *was* restricted, even in broad daylight. Riding the footplate of a southbound train some 40 years later, signalling expert O.S. Nock noted that, although the driver of the troop train enjoyed an unrestricted view ahead along a three-mile straight right up to the road bridge at Quintinshill, immediately after that there was a curve, and any vehicles in the loop would obscure the existence of the local train facing north on the wrong line.

Following the St. Bedes accident in County Durham only seven months after Quintinshill, the reporting officer did recommend the installation of track circuiting at that particular junction. The cause of the accident – inattention to the job in hand by footplate staff and, more particularly, a signalman – was uneasily similar to the Caledonian accident, and confirms that both accidents could have been averted had track circuiting been installed to offer technical protection to the railway's innocent passengers. Blaming errant railway staff for an accident is often the easy way out for management, or for politicians and it still goes on in this age of privatised railways.

Passenger Carriages

Biggar.

From the start of its operations in 1848, the Caledonian was noted for the quality of its passenger vehicles. When First and Second Class travellers joined the very first train to leave Glasgow for the south, on 15 February 1848, they found four-wheel carriages 18 feet long which 'are in every way handsome and commodious … [First Class] are painted lake colour on the outside, and highly varnished. Inside they are 5 ft 10 inches high and each department [compartment] is six feet by seven in dimension. They are fitted up in blue colour, cloth on the cushions, morocco elbows, silk window blinds and layings, and Brussels carpet … the wood work is mahogany highly polished, and the topsides and roof are covered with cream coloured oilcloth. Above the window, strips of stained glass have been introduced, which give the carriages a light and cheerful appearance.'

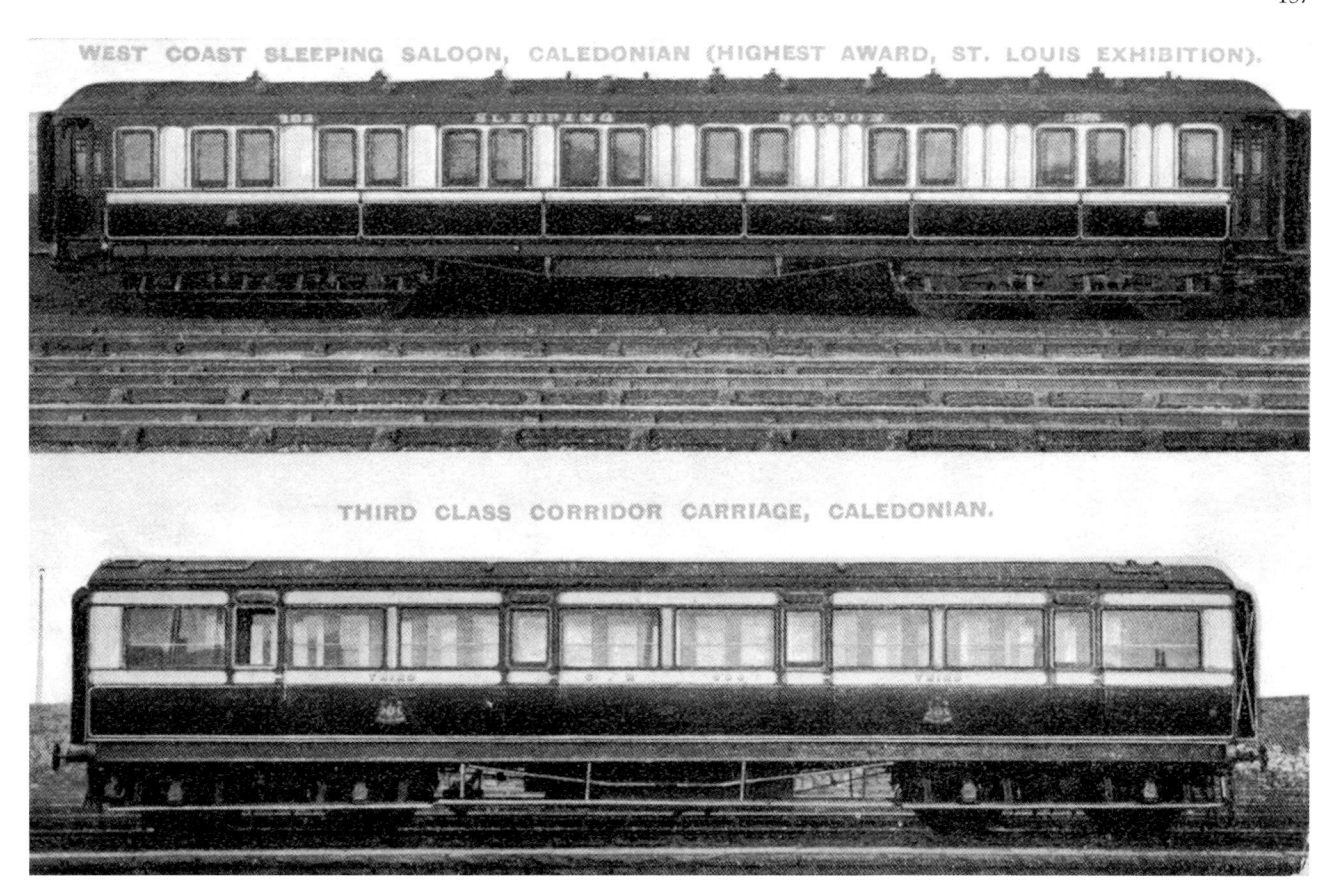

WEST COAST SLEEPING SALOON, CALEDONIAN (HIGHEST AWARD, ST. LOUIS EXHIBITION).

THIRD CLASS CORRIDOR CARRIAGE, CALEDONIAN.

So reported the Glasgow Herald correspondent on his return trip to Beattock. Accommodation for Third Class passengers was presumably not included in the special train, and one historian has described such vehicles as 'open bone-shakers on wheels'. Sleeping car services were introduced on the West Coast Route in October 1873, although the NBR had managed to pre-empt the 'Caley' – and its own East Coast allies – pioneering (British) sleeping services earlier that year. There is archival evidence however, that the initiative for this came from the Manchester company, Ashbury Ltd (later part of the Metro-Cammel group) which had demonstrated a proprietary six-wheel, two-berth, sleeping car to both the CR and the NBR in the spring of that year. The NBR placed its order first, while the 'Caley' waited until later in the year for its southern partner, the LNWR, to work up an interest.

The Caledonian's record in passenger vehicle provision really began to take on an unmatchable lustre at the beginning of the 20th Century. In 1902, new Third Class carriages, 50 feet in length, were designed by McIntosh with centre gangways, and were considered in advance of everything else available to the economy-minded traveller at that time. Three years later, McIntosh excelled himself with his 'Grampian' vehicles.

High Blantyre.

Broughton.

Designed for the services between Glasgow, Edinburgh, and Aberdeen, the new vehicles were 68 feet in length, running on 12 wheels, and built up to the limit of the loading gauge. There were toilets at each end of the non-braked vehicles, the latter containing bicycle racks, safes for the storage of valuables, and electrical switches to control heating and lighting. First Class passengers to and from Aberdeen (10 am out of Buchanan Street, 9.25 am from Princes Street), relaxed on brown tapestry moquette cushions trimmed with silk vellum lace. Woodwork was polished walnut, and cashmere rugs lay beneath the travellers' feet.

Busby Viaduct.

If this seemed to be the height of luxury, the Caledonian had still more to offer its long-distance travellers. Just before the outbreak of World War One, the 'Caley' came to an agreement with the Pullman Company for the operation of these luxury vehicles on certain routes. These were unique in Scotland – while the NBR and GSWR ran Anglo-Scottish trains incorporating American-style Pullman coaches, these were contracted by the Midland Railway. Reference has already been made to the Maid of Morven, the Pullman observation car, with its unique bay window at one end, giving magnificent views on the Glasgow-Oban run, but other services also benefitted. There were no fewer than six buffet cars, four of them charmingly named after the four ladies-in-waiting to Mary Stewart, Queen of Scots.

Pullmans were run on four daily services in each direction between Edinburgh and Glasgow, five on Saturdays. Some of these trains stopped at West Calder and Shotts, so it was not just tourists in the Highlands who could sample Pullman luxury on a Caledonian train. A supplement was payable to use these coaches (1/6 from Glasgow to Callander), but tickets for Pullman trains could even be purchased at any wayside station, when changing to a Pullman-equipped service later in the journey. What a pity that wartime conditions interceded to reduce the publicity value of these elite services.

Maid of Morven, Stirling.

No 2. Royal Naval Ambulance Train 1918

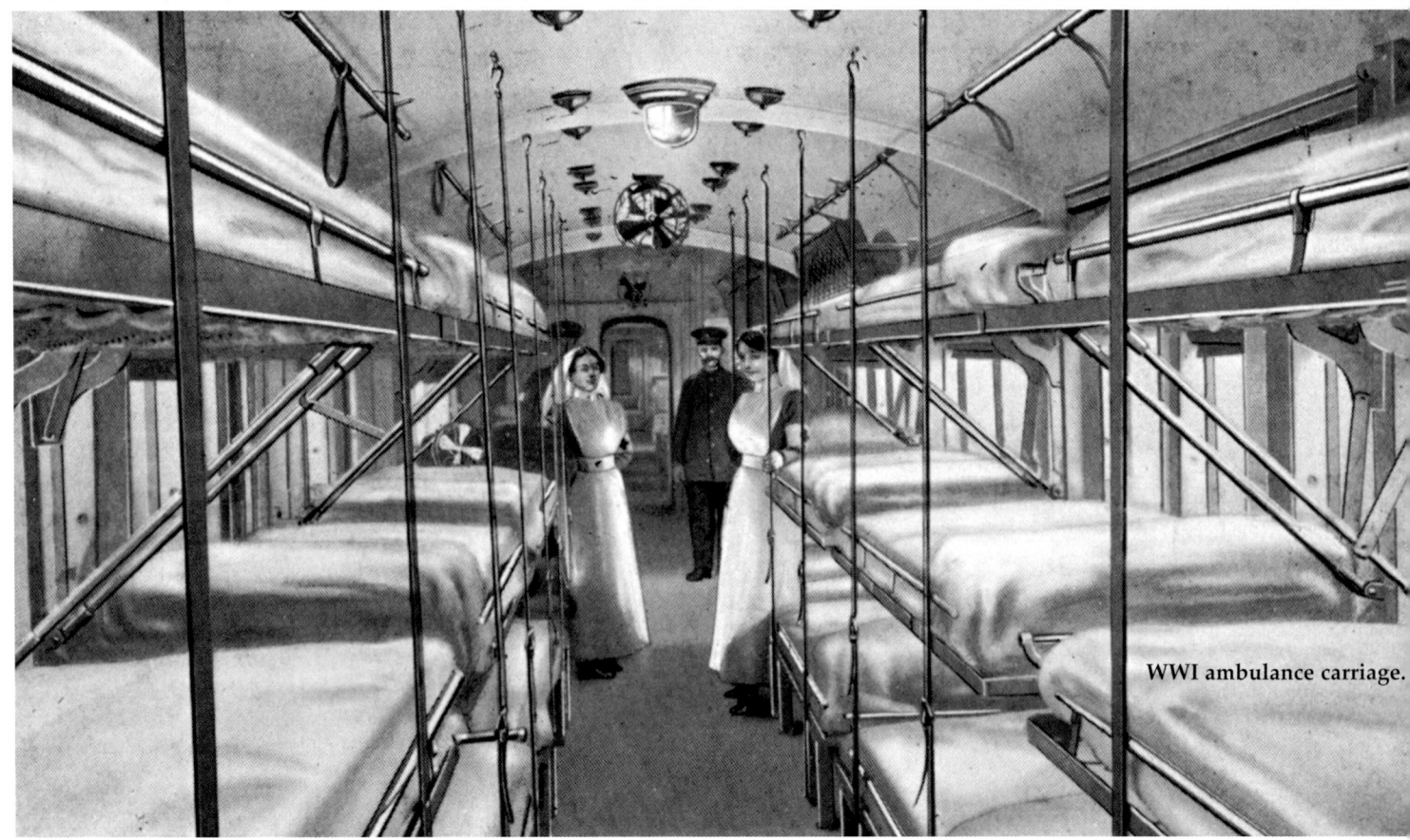

WWI ambulance carriage.

Ardrossan.

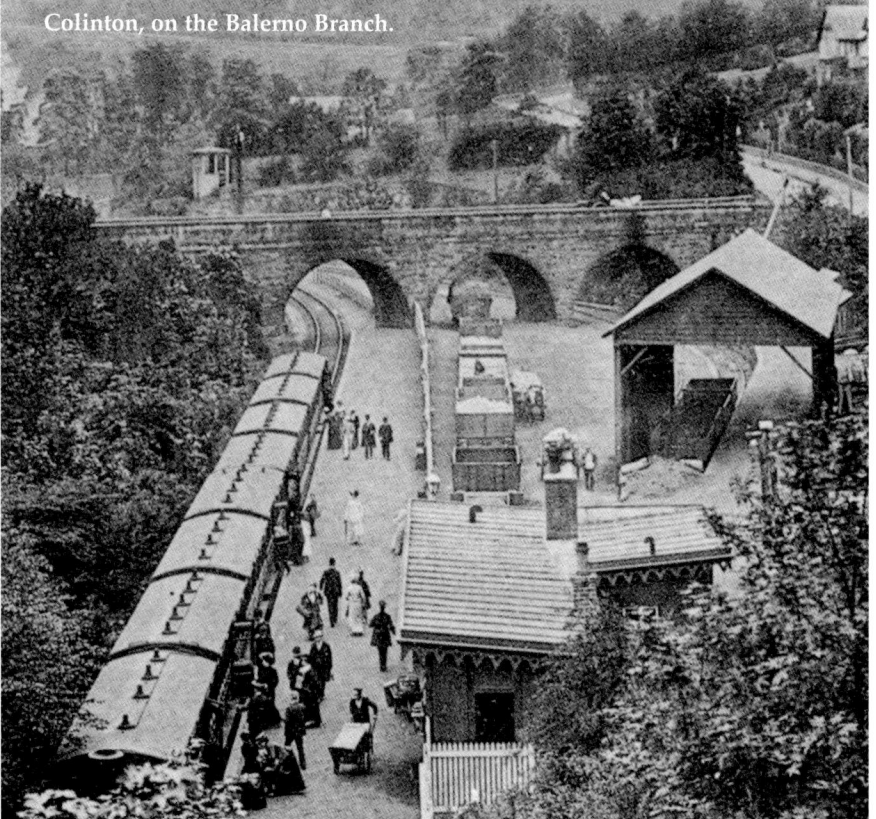

Colinton, on the Balerno Branch.

The history of Caledonian Railway passenger vehicles is neatly, and surprisingly, 'book ended' with the delivery in 1922 of coaches for Edinburgh suburban services by Pickering of Wishaw. Like those vehicles on the 1848 'press trip' from Glasgow to Beattock and back, these were four-wheelers, surely the last to be built new for a British passenger service. Designed for operation on the sinuous Balerno Branch, these were only some ten feet longer, at 28 ft, than the 1848 batch.

Weighing only 15 tons each, the First Class vehicles were finished in mahogany stained walnut, while the ceilings had 'Lincrusta' ornamental borders. Carpets were of velvet pile, upholstery was moquette, and door interiors finished in embossed leather. Third Class passengers had to slum it with mahogany finishings and lino on the floor. These trains were still running after World War Two, although the service they had been designed for had succumbed to tram and bus competition. One wonders if those road vehicles offered quite the same amenities as the train.

Steamers

Galatea

Ship operation did not present most Scottish rail companies with any kind of new challenge. From the first decade of passenger-carrying operations on Scotland's main lines, the railway companies, particularly the NBR were having to come to terms with the demands of topography, particularly the need to cross rivers and estuaries (called 'Firths' in Scotland) by ferry-boat. In contrast, having been conceived as a kind of 'Grand Junction' line, the Caledonian was more internalised, and less immediately involved in ferry crossing as an integral part of its network.

Yet, when the Edwardian era dawned as the Golden Age of Clyde steamers, the three Scottish railways operating on the Firth of Clyde owned no less than two-thirds of the entire fleet. The Caledonian, needless to say, claimed the fastest and most elegantly-decorated vessels on the Clyde.

Wemyss Bay, Duchess of Rothsey.

Wemyss Bay, original station.

The 'Caley' first met the sea with its takeover of the Glasgow, Paisley, and Greenock Railway in 1851, working originally in connection with the Bute Steam Packet Company, but the rail concern soon took on a more direct control of maritime operations. The setting up of the Caledonian Steam Packet Company, a separate legal entity from the Caledonian Railway, did not take place until 1889, although Caledonian colours were 'weel kent' on the Clyde long before then, with Gourock, Wemyss Bay, and Ardrossan all becoming active bases for the company's ships. Wemyss Bay was the result of a working agreement – although effectively a takeover – of the Wemyss Bay Railway in 1865, and resulted in the conversion of the original, workaday, buildings at Wemyss Bay itself, into a truly remarkable station concourse whose circular glazed roof covered the booking-hall and walkway to the quayside. This, the product of architect James Miller, is still regarded as one of the finest examples of station architecture anywhere in the UK.

Gourock.

Gourock, fully operational as a meeting-place of train and steamer from 1890, was more utilitarian, but no less expensive. The tunnel to the shore was such a logistical challenge to the Caledonian that it was actually abandoned in 1869. The successful completion of the line prompted the creation of the Caledonian Steam Packet Company. The Caledonian now felt itself to be in an ideal position to challenge the dominance of the GSWR fleet, while the NBR largely kept to itself on the north bank of the Clyde.

The new operating company standardised its colours as buff funnels, navy blue (later black) hulls and with the paddles boxes painted in white and decorated with gold outlining. Needless to say, a red lion rampant on a yellow background – a standard normally reserved for the royal family when living in Scotland – was cheerfully appropriated for the design of the pennant.

By 1906 the company was operating turbine vessels, the pride of the fleet being the Duchess of Argyll, claimed to be the fastest steamer on the Clyde. She had a distinguished record in two world wars, her civilian record lasting to 1952, when she was sold to the Admiralty, her new owners not disposing of her until the end of the 1960s.

Duchess of Argyll.

Balloch Pier, with passengers boarding the Princess May.

The Caledonian was rightly proud of its maritime activities, and devoted considerable resources to servicing them, not least in the provision of connecting rail services from Glasgow Central. These served a double market, with an increasing number of better-off families moving out of the city and creating commuter communities along the Clyde Coast. A number of larger locomotive classes were employed on Clyde Coast trains, the most interesting of them being Pickersgill's 'Pacific' tanks of 1917, although the largest 4-6-0s could also be found on these trains.

There was no chance that the Caledonian would allow the North British to have Loch Lomond all to itself. Through joint ownership of the Dumbarton & Balloch Railway, the Caledonian was able to ensure a presence on the loch from 1896, although this resulted in wasteful duplication of services for quite some time.

The Caledonian was also responsible for the steamer services on Loch Tay, reached by the Killin Branch off the Callander & Oban in 1886. The Caledonian Steam Packet Company did not formally take over these sailings until 1922, the principal vessel on the loch being the Queen of the Lake, the last steamer to operate there when World War Two brought services to an end in 1939. Services on Loch Awe, which the Caledonian Steam Packet Company interested itself from 1922 (thereby falling outside the scope of this book) also ended with the opening of Hitler's War. Scottish steamer operation, whether on firth or loch, was never to be the same again.

Loch Tay Pier, Lady of the Lake (left), Queen of the Lake (right).

Docks

The Caledonian Railway was less active in dock and harbour ownership than its main rival, the North British. It owned fewer dock installations than the other company, but one which did come under Caledonian control was the most valuable railway-controlled harbour anywhere in northern Britain.

Grangemouth Harbour came into the Caledonian's possession through its takeover in 1865 of the Scottish Central Railway, along with the Forth & Clyde Canal. The rail company was shrewd enough to realise that Grangemouth was worth investing in – it offered trade connections with Continental ports, while being situated much closer to west of Scotland markets than Leith, and with a canal connection to the west for bulk cargoes, if required. Within 15 years the Caledonian had created the Carron Dock at Grangemouth, with a water surface area of 20 acres, and in 1906 the Grange Dock was opened. This was 50% bigger again, and was 26 feet deep. At the same time a new sea-lock 626 feet long and no less than 80 feet wide, was provided, with three pairs of steel gates.

OLD DOCK, GRANGEMOUTH

So important did Grangemouth become for general cargoes (and it still is), that it also fostered a petrochemical industry, becoming Scotland's most important trade and industry complex of the present day. The 'Caley' even hedged its bets by acquiring running-powers over the NBR into nearby Bo'ness, although that port was soon completely outperformed by its neighbour a couple of miles to the west. Westwards along the Forth & Clyde Canal, the Caledonian owned harbour facilities at the (land-locked) Port Dundas in Glasgow, and at Bowling on the Clyde. Here the eastern part of the latter harbour was owned by the company, allowing the transshipment of cargoes between marine vessels and canal or rail.

Harbour facilities at Oban were part-owned by the Caledonian (through the Callander & Oban Railway) and at Stranraer – the former now a vital part of the roll-on/roll off meeting of road and ferry – as well as at Kentallen (Ballachulish) and Wemyss Bay. On Loch Lomond, Balloch Pier was jointly owned with the rival North British.

The major ports of Glasgow, Leith, and Granton were all served by the Caledonian; indeed Granton was one of the earliest points where the 'Caley' met the sea, and through the port's ownership by the Duke of Buccleuch, long a 'Caley' supporter, more attention was paid to Granton initially than to Leith. The company did not send locomotives into Leith Docks until 1867 (four years before the NBR), but within ten years the Leith Dock Commission felt it necessary to draw up guidelines for their use.

Glasgow Docks.

Now preserved in the National Archives of Scotland, the Leith Dock Commission guidelines are worth examining, as they draw attention to a facet of railroading which has practically vanished. These operating rules made clear that locomotive operations would be conducted 'only during the pleasure of the Commissioners', and the locomotives would have to be 'small and light'. Coke was the only fuel they could consume, and an 'iron grating' or other form of spark arrester had to be fitted. No train in and out of the docks could exceed 30 wagons, while 10 was the limit for trains travelling exclusively within the complex. These could not exceed a speed of 3 mph, except in the case of coal trains travelling between the hoists and the Seafield yards to the east, in which case 8 mph was permissible. Each train had to be accompanied by 'qualified engine pilots' wearing red caps.

Bowling Harbour.

Arbroath Harbour.

Montrose Harbour.

Within 30 years (by 1907) a new code of rules was drafted, the CR appendices to the working timetables having to be modified as a result. Archival records show that J.F. McIntosh, no less, was brought into the discussion concerning the adoption of these rules, and he asked Inspector Ballantyne, based at Merchiston Station (some miles from the sea), if the CR engines working the docks met the specifications. On 29 October, Ballantyne sent a memo to McIntosh, assuring him that the locos allocated to this work were all 'quite suitable', although there was a recurring problem with bearing springs hung below the axle boxes on the pugs. These were snagging guard rails and causeway blocks, Ballantyne suggesting that this problem be corrected when the engines went through shops.

Leith Dock Commission files show that the Caledonian was a persistent offender in rule-breaking, regularly loading above agreed limits and sometimes abandoning trains in mid-journey even although this inevitably caused inconvenience to other dock users. One letter of complaint from a shipping line points out that a train was left standing on a swing bridge while the engine was used to shunt wagons forward in a coal hoist. Ship loading at Leith was frequently held up by trains taking too long to negotiate busy quays, where, naturally, all loading and unloading had to stop. There was an implication that the engine crews and stevedores were in cahoots; since the latter were employed on a casual daily basis, the slowing-down of work was directly in their interest and they may have promised engine-crews a drink for slow passage through the dock system. Perhaps management could have devised a more dignified way of employing people and thus accelerated productivity. The NBR was not named in these complaints nearly as frequently as the Caledonian and its successor, the LMS. Make of that what you will.

Dock and harbour facilities at Aberdeen, Arbroath, Montrose (reached by a branch), Perth, and Dundee, were also served by the Caledonian, as were Ayr, Ardrossan, Troon, Greenock, Port Glasgow, Paisley and Renfrew. One firth which was not served directly by the Caledonian was the Solway – instead the estuary was spanned by a viaduct, and the 'Caley' did not follow the North British in expanding into England.

Hotels

Central Station Hotel, Glasgow.

Princes Street, Edinburgh.

For a company which always realised the need for positive publicity – playing a spectacular part in the Races to the North, issuing postcards to illustrate its prettiest landscape views (and its role in the Race to the North) – the Caledonian was slow to enter the hotel industry. Scotland's smaller rail companies were more active in this aspect of tourism, which would appear to be a logical partner to the passenger transport business. Yet when the Caledonian, somewhat belatedly, began to take a serious interest in hotel management, it constructed three major establishments.

Its flagship was the Central Hotel in Glasgow, built next to, and above, the terminus of that name in 1885. With 221 bedrooms, this was among the largest establishments in Scotland, but is architecturally undistinguished, being partly converted from offices. Extensive structural precautions were taken against fire, and the hotel opened with electric lighting from the start. It featured in Evelyn Waugh's novel *Officers and Gentlemen*, where a vital link in the plot falls into place. Like all transport hotels, Central Hotel is now privately owned.

Princes Street Hotel, Grand Stair.

Princes Street Hotel, Lounge.

Princes Street Hotel.

More notable in architectural terms is the Caledonian Hotel in Edinburgh. This was opened as the 'Princes Street Hotel' in 1903, although its location, built over the company's terminus, is technically in Rutland Street. Its red Dumfriesshire stonework stands out in a city mainly built of Craigleith sandstone, but its reputation as a first-rate establishment has followed it into private ownership. When the Commonwealth Heads of Government conference was held in the capital in 1992, this was the base for the British Prime Minister.

Perthshire was the location for what was supposed to be greatest 'Caley' hotel of all. The Gleneagles establishment, with 210 bedrooms, almost as many as the company's two major hotels – was designed (on the drawing-boards from 1913 onwards) to cater for the growing interest in golf as both a participatory and a spectator sport. Even before World War One, the CR timetables carried pages of adverts of golfing resorts. Yet Gleneagles was not opened until 1924, when the Caledonian Railway had ceased to exist, quickly becoming one of the jewels in the crown of the new LMS company. If the Caley appears to have lost a business opportunity here, the golfing centre of Gleneagles at least acquired a prestige railway hotel long before St. Andrews – it was left to British Transport Hotels to open one there as late as 1968 – with the local railway about to close.

The only other location for a Caledonian hotel was Perth, where the company co-owned the Station Hotel with the Highland Railway and the NBR. Despite operating into both Aberdeen and Carlisle, the Caledonian opened no hotels in either city; in contrast the Great North of Scotland Railway owned two in Aberdeen, and Carlisle County Hotel was let out to private operators by the LNWR. The hotel industry seems to have been something of a missed opportunity for the Caledonian Railway, which didn't usually miss many of those.

Gleneagles Hotel.

The End of the Caledonian Railway

Staff, probably at Perth Station.

While World War One ended in victory for the United Kingdom and her allies in 1918, it brought near-disaster for many of the country's railway companies. All of them had found the logistical and manpower demands of the First World War to be almost insurmountable. A couple of amalgamations resulted in England, but the most lasting effect of the War was that companies and their staff became accustomed – as did the civilian population – to the effects of government control. Railway activities during the conflict had been co-ordinated, and to a considerable extent, controlled, through the UK Board of Trade and its agency, the Railway Executive. There was a general feeling that things could not go on as they had in the piping days of Edwardian peace. Nationalisation was an operational possibility, but the Labour movement was not yet strong enough to achieve what it managed in 1948; the Liberal party had formed the government for some 12 years before the war, and its leader, Lloyd George, called and won a 'khaki election' in December 1918. His Minister of Transport was an ambitious ex–North Eastern Railway official called Sir Eric Geddes, a strong supporter of centralising railway control. The result was a Railways Bill, drafted largely by him and introduced into Parliament in 1921. This proposed the establishment of four major groupings of railway and was to be the death-knell of the Caledonian Railway Company.

The 'Caley' did not go down without a fight. Whether the challenge was worth the effort put into it, is questionable, but the fact remains that the Caledonian was one of only two railways which remained independent after the Act became law on 1 January 1923. Along with the North Staffordshire Railway, the Caledonian formally disputed the terms of amalgamation. It was, however, prepared to accept £886,249 from the government for 'arrears of maintenance and renewals of ways and works', out of a total national disbursement of £25 million.

What its shareholders could not accept was that the company's own valuation at the Grouping should be based on the trading year 1913, ten years earlier. On the face of it, this was not an ungenerous calculation – most of the UK's railways enjoyed considerable prosperity until the outbreak of war, but since the Caledonian's stock structure was different from most other concerns, this apparently reasonable offer was deemed unacceptable, and the 'Caley' decided to take the matter before an Amalgamation Tribunal, as it had a legal right to do.

No expense was spared in preparing for this crunch meeting, scheduled for June 1923, the company retaining two distinguished legal advisers – Sir John Simon, a former Home Secretary, and Hugh Pattison Macmillan, soon to be Lord Advocate and later Baron Macmillan. In the meantime 'all our principal officers have been appointed to the new organisation. We are glad to know that their merits have been recognised', the Caledonian informed the Railway Times. The company spokesman added that, meantime, the 'Caley' operated as part of the new Group.

So the Caledonian Railway joined the London Midland and Scottish Railway Group, along with the London & North Western (with the Lancashire & Yorkshire), the Midland, the Furness, the Highland, and, much to its chagrin, the aforesaid Glasgow & South Western. Unlike the North British – and probably because of the delay caused by its contesting of amalgamation conditions – the Caledonian failed to have the same influence on the new super-company as the NBR did on the nascent LNER and the NBR's Chairman William Whitelaw headed the new company for its first 15 years.

Staff at Strathaven North.

In retrospect, it is so disappointing that CR shareholders disputed the terms of the 1923 Grouping, preventing the 'Caley' from taking what could have been a leading role in the newly-forming LMS company, particularly with the new company suffering immediately from rivalry, indeed almost deadly enmity, between the new leading 'partners', the LNWR and the Midland. A strong third voice could easily have become an influential one, ensuring, if nothing else, that a devolved administrative structure was created, and a more sensible traction policy adopted. In particular, the idea of the LMS perpetuating a fleet of underpowered Midland 4-4-0s in the mid-1920s, while the LNER built Pacifics, showed a serious lack of forward thinking. The LMS was soon to develop an over-centralised structure, where even the drafting of posters had to be approved by 'Euston'. Again, in contrast, the LNER immediately divided its network into Areas with 'Area General Managers' enjoying considerable devolution of powers. Perhaps this could have been attempted on the West Coast system if the 'Caley' had played a more central role in administrative planning when the new group was still forming.

Approved by the government from the start, its prospectus published at Westminster in 1844, the Caledonian Railway ended its existence in conflict with London, and all to no avail. It was a disappointingly negative end to a company which had been conceived so imaginatively, as an integral part of a national transport network.

Planned with flair and operated with panache, it had earned the accolade of 'The' Caledonian Railway. Now it was no more.

Kilbirnie, 1936.

Inchture, 1941.

Solway Viaduct Bowness end, 2005.

WORKS CONSULTED

Wherever possible, primary records have been consulted, including Caledonian Railway company papers, particularly BR/CAL/1/1 onwards and the BR/CAL/8 sequence. Also researched were the Solway Junction Railway, Cathcart District Railway, and Leith Dock Commission archives – all these were examined in the West Search Room of the National Archives of Scotland at Charlotte Square, Edinburgh, whose staff are thanked for their helpfulness.

Secondary sources.

Carter, Oliver. *An Illustrated History of British Railway Hotels 1838-1983*. Silver Link, 1990.
Highet, Campbell. *Scottish Locomotive History: 1831-1923*. Allen & Unwin, 1970.
Johnston, Colin and Hume, John R. *Glasgow Stations*. David & Charles, 1979.
Kernahan, Jack. *The Cathcart Circle*. SRPS, 1980.
Marshall, Peter F. *The Scottish Central Railway. Perth to Stirling*. Oakwood, 1998.
Middlemass, T. *The 'Scottish' 4-4-0; its place in railway history*. Atlantic, 1994.
Mullay, A.J. *Rail Centres – Edinburgh*. Ian Allan, 1991.
Mullay, A.J. *Rails across the Border*. PSL, 1990.
Nock, O.S. *The Caledonian Railway*. Ian Allan, 1963.
Robertson, C.J.A. *The Origins of the Scottish Railway System 1722-1844*. John Donald, 1983.
Rolt, L.T.C. *Red for Danger*. 4th edition. David & Charles, 1982.
Smith, W.A.C. and Anderson, P. *An Illustrated History of Glasgow's Railways*. Irwell, 1993.
Thomas, J. *The Callander and Oban Railway*. David & Charles, 1966.
Thomas, J. *A Regional History of the Railways of Great Britain. Vol. 6. The Lowlands and Borders*.
   (Revised by A.J.S. Paterson). David St. John Thomas, 1984.
Thomas, J. and Turnock, D. *A Regional History of the Railways of Great Britain. Vol.15. The North of Scotland*.
   2nd edition. David St. John Thomas, 1993.
Also, various copies of the Journal of the Caledonian Railway Association from 1984. (Journal later entitled 'The True Line')

The author wishes to thank the Lord Lyon, King of Arms, for his prompt and courteous attention to an enquiry about the CR's heraldic devices. Thanks are also due to the staff of the National Library of Scotland and of Edinburgh City Libraries. Thanks also to Richard Stenlake, whose collection forms the majority of the pictorial material. Allan Brochie provided the pictures of Moffat, Addiewell, and Dundee West station; Guthrie Hutton for the picture of the Kelvin Aqueduct in Maryhill. and to John Biggart for the upper of the Beith Town accidents. Lastly thanks to Lewis Hutton who provided the picture of Partick Central and the map of the proposed line to Ayr, and who wrote the Lanarkshire Water schemes section and the extended picture captions.

Princes Street, locomotive decorated for driver's wedding day.

PICTURE INDEX
Locomotives

Number Name	Wheel Configuration	Build Year		Number Name	Wheel Configuration	Build Year	
8	2-4-0	1870	126	248	0-4-2	1864	42
17	4-4-0	1894	83	354	0-6-0	1884	45
24	2-4-0	1870	156	424	0-4-4T	1907	15
30	2-4-0	1872	44	436	2-4-0	1867	42
33	2-4-0	1872	158	439	0-4-4T	1900	102
46	2-4-0	1874	85	447	0-4-4T	1900	80
50, Sir James Thompson	4-6-0	1903	82	448	0-4-4T	1900	109
52	2-4-0	1874	5	492	0-8-0T	1903	112
52	4-6-0	1905	15	578	0-6-0	1896	121
54	4-6-0	1905	90	600	0-8-0	1901	112
66	4-4-0	1884	22	683	0-6-0	1884	67
72	4-4-0	1884	45	721, Dunalastair	4-4-0	1896	110
76	4-4-0	1889	156	731	4-4-0	1896	71
77	4-4-0	1889	18	746	0-6-0	1897	110
83	4-4-0	1891	135	769	4-4-0	1898	141
87	2-2-2	1865	41	780	4-4-0	1898	111
100	2-4-0	1867	41	784	0-6-0T	1898	112
117	4-4-0	1912	38	822	0-6-0	1899	82
123	4-2-2	1886	46	857	0-6-0	1900	2
124, Eglinton	4-4-0	1886	27	888	4-4-0	1900	15
127	4-4-0	1876	43	893	4-4-0	1900	111
14?	4-4-0	1904/5	19	901	4-4-0	1899	9
147	2-4-0T	1879	44	902	4-4-0	1899	5
149	4-4-0	1905	130	903, Carndean	4-6-0	1906	147
163	0-4-4T	1915	114	904	4-6-0	1906	18
172	0-4-4T	1884	62, 63	904	4-6-0	1906	113
181	4-4-0	1882	98	918	4-6-0	1906	8
181	4-6-0	1914	113	953	4-6-2T	1917	122
185	4-6-0	1914	114	955	4-6-2T	1917	1
194	0-4-4T	1891	10	1167	0-4-4WT	1873	43, 109
230	0-4-4-T	1886	136	1231	0-4-4T	1886	131

Oban, looking west.

Stations and Places

Abington	12
Aberdeen	135
Addiewell	22
Airdrie staff	26
Airth	39
Alloa Swing Bridge	40
Alloa Swing Bridge accident	155
Almond Bank*	92, 109, 178

Almond Bank.

Alyth Junction	130, 136		Benderloch	106
Arbroath	144		Biggar	47, 156
Arbroath Harbour	168		Bishopton	117
Ardrossan	161		Blackford	87
Ardrossan (Montgomerie Pier)	123		Blackwood	80
Auchterhouse	138		Bothwell staff	26
Auldbar Road	131		Bowling	116
Baldovan	139		Bowling Harbour	167
Baldragon	138		Bowness on Solway	60, 175
Balerno	73		Brayton Junction	61
Ballachuilish	98, 107			
Baillieston	25			
Balloch	116			
Balloch Pier	165			
Balquhidder	101, 102			
Bankfoot	136			
Barnhill (Dundee)	143			
Barnton	92			
Beattock Station	10			
Beattock Summit	2, 8			
Beith Town, accident	152			
Bellshill	24			

* The village name is Almondbank, the station was called Almond Bank.

Brechin	145
Bridge Street	29
Bromfield	61
Broughton	47, 158
Buchanan Street	15, 27
Busby	69
Busby Viaduct	159
Callander	98, 100
Cambuslang	85
Camps Water Scheme	54, 55
Cardonald	1
Carlisle	4
Carlisle, Port Carlisle Junction	4
Carluke	13
Carnoustie	88
Carnwath	16
Carstairs	13, 15, 28
Carstairs, flooding	152
Central Station (Glasgow)	86, 96, 146, 147, 169
Chapelhall	25
Clarkston	68
Clydebank	115
Coalburn	64
Coatbridge	14
Cobbinshaw	17
Colinton	72, 161
Connel Bridge	91, 104, 106
Coulter Water Scheme	56, 57
Coupar Angus	129
Coupar Angus, accident	149
Crawford, accident	151
Creagan Viaduct	107

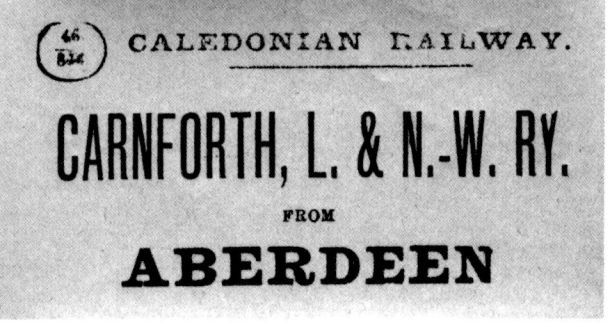

Caledonian Steam Packet Company's New Turbine Steamer "DUCHESS OF ARGYLL," now Sailing Daily between Ardrossan and the Island of Arran.

Crianlarich	103
Crieff	109
Crieff Junction (Gleneagles)	87
Cumbernauld	33
Dalserf	79
Dalveen Pass	8
Denny	39
Dolphinton	49
Doune	99
Drumlithie	89
Drumlithie summit	132
Drummelzier	50
Dubton Junction	131
Duchess of Argyll	164
Duchess of Hamilton	95
Duchess of Rothsey	162
Dunblane	36
Dundee West	140
Dundee, Dundee and Newtyle Terminus	140
Dunlop	126
Dunsyre	49
East Kilbride	70
Ecclefechan	8
Edzell	145
Eglinton Street	85
Elvanfoot	11
Fauldhouse	22
Fordoun	132
Fort Matilda	120
Forteviot	37
Friockheim	143
Galatea	162
Garnkirk	14
Garnqueen	32
Georgetown	117

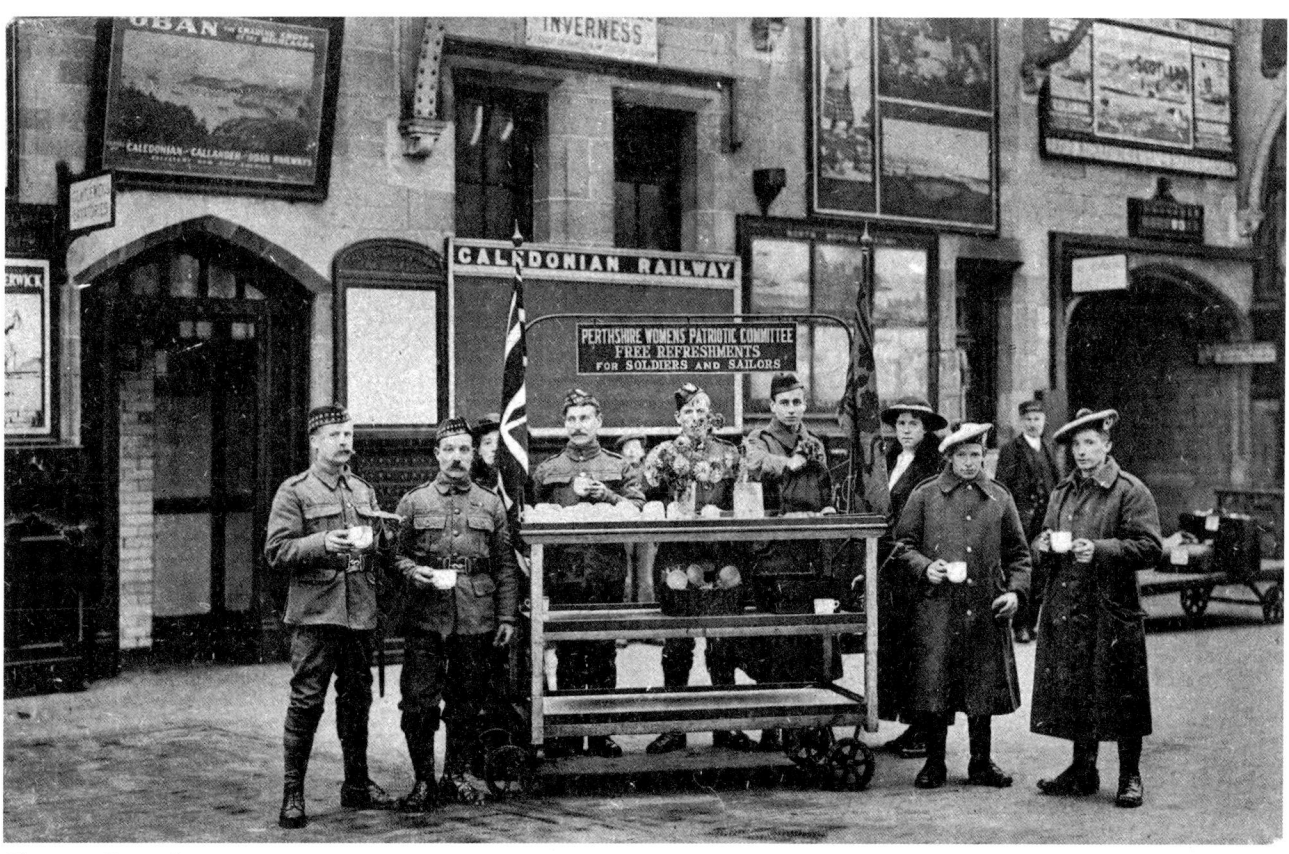

Glasgow Central	86, 96, 146, 147 169
Glasgow Cross	65
Glasgow Docks	167
Glassford	75
Glenboig	32, 33
Gleneagles (Crieff Junction)	87
Gleneagles Hotel	171
Gourock	120, 164

Invergowrie	141
Inverkip	121
Irvine	124
Isla Valley	130
Jerviston Viaduct	24
Juniper Green	73
Kelvinbridge	66
Kilbirnie	175
Killin Junction	102
Kingsknowe	18
Kirkbride Junction	60
Kirkpatrick	7
Kirriemuir	142
Kirtlebridge	59
Kirtlebridge, accident	150
Lady of the Lake	165
Langbank	118

Gourock Pier	94
Grangemouth Docks	166
Granton	71
Greenhill	34
Greenock Central	119
Greenock Upper	121
Greenock West	119
Gretna	7
Gretna Green, (Quintinshill) disaster	153, 154
Hamilton	76
High Blantyre	74, 158
Inchture	127, 142, 175

Important Notice.

FROM 1st April till 30th September, the 10 a.m. Corridor Luncheon Car Express from London (Euston) has Through Carriages to Gourock, and Direct Steamers run from that point to Rothesay, Craigmore, Dunoon, Innellan, Kilcreggan, Cove, Blairmore, Strone, Ardnadam, Kilmun, Hunter's Quay, Kirn, Toward, &c., thus enabling Passengers from London to these places completing the journey, with only one change, viz., from Train to Steamer.

Passengers from Birmingham, Liverpool, Manchester, Cardiff, Bristol, and the West of England by the West Coast Route to Glasgow and the Clyde Coast Resorts have similar Conveniences.

Larbert	34, 44
Larbert, accident	149
Larkhall	77
Laurencekirk	89, 132
Leadhills	62, 63
Leith, cross Leith line	72
Lesmahagow	80, 93
Loch Tay Pier	103, 165
Lochearnhead	108
Lochee West	139
Lockerbie	9, 84, 184
Lothian Road	30
Luncarty	128
Magdalen Green	141
Maid of Morven	101, 159
Maryhill	67
Maryhill, Dawsholm	67
Marykirk	89
Methven	109
Mid Calder	18
Mid Calder Staff	17
Moffat	10, 11
Montgomerie Pier (Ardrossan)	123
Montrose Harbour	168
Motherwell	84
Mount Florida	68
Muchals	134
Muirkirk	64
Newmains	25
Newtyle New Station	137
Newtyle Old Station	137
Oban	91, 97, 105, 177
Omoa	24
Partick Central	66
Peebles	48
Perth	38, 88, 181
Perth Moncrieff Tunnel	37, 38
Port Glasgow	118
Portlethan	134
Princes Street	19, 30, 86, 96, 148, 169, 170, 171, 176
Princess May	165
Queen of the Lake	165
Quintinshill, disaster	153, 154
Rosemount	136
Saltcoats	124
Shotts	23

TOUR TO TROSSACHS, LOCH KATRINE AND LOCH LOMOND

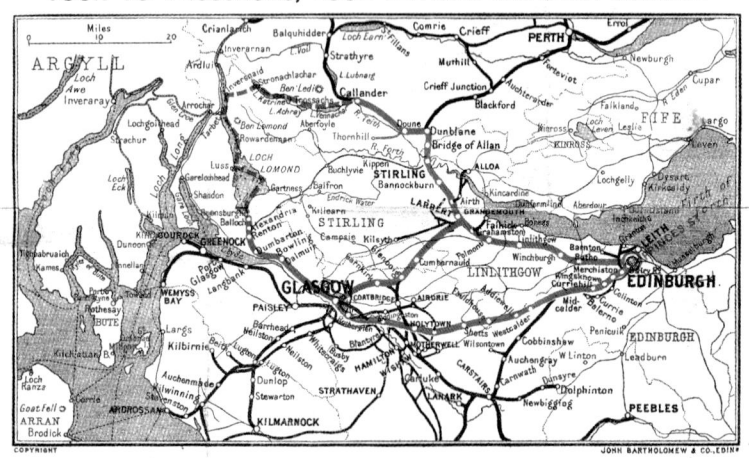

SCOTLAND'S PREMIER TOUR.

The Trossachs, Loch Katrine Via CALLANDER **and Loch Lomond**

Frequent Express Train Service from

EDINBURGH (Princes Street) and GLASGOW (Buchanan Street)

Going via CALLANDER, returning via BALLOCH.

Also from

EDINBURGH (Princes Street) and GLASGOW (Central Low Level)

Going via BALLOCH, returning via CALLANDER.

FARES.

	1st Class & Cabin.	3rd Class & Cabin.
Edinburgh (Princes Street),	26/2	19/6
Glasgow (Buchanan St. or Central),	18/11	15/10

NOTE.—The route via Callander is the only one by which Tourists can follow the chase as described in "The Lady of the Lake," and no Coaches other than those which run from and to Callander Station pass through "The Trossachs."

CALEDONIAN RAILWAY.
SHREWSBURY FROM **PERTH.**

CALEDONIAN RAILWAY.
NEWPORT, MON. FROM **PERTH**

Thorntonhall.

Solway Viaduct	58, 59, 175
South Alloa	40
St. Rollox	27
St. Fillans	108
Stanley	129
Stepps	15
Stewarton	126
Stirling	35, 159
Stobo	48
Stonehaven	133
Stonehouse	78
Strathaven Central	79
Strathaven North	75
Strathaven viaducts	78, 93
Strathord	128
Strathyre	101
Symington	12
Talla Reservoir	51, 52, 53
Taynuilt	90, 104
Thankerton	12
Thankerton, accident	151
Thorntonhall	70, 183
Tillietudlem	79
Uplawmoor	127
Wamphray	9
Wanlockhead	62
Wemyss Bay	94
Wemyss Bay new station	163
Wemyss Bay old station	163
Wemyss Bay Pier	122, 162
West Calder	20, 21
Whifflet	13
Wilsontown	16

LONDON AND NORTH-WESTERN AND CALEDONIAN RAILWAYS

Saloon or Family Carriages

Can be arranged for the conveyance of Family Parties between all parts of England and Scotland on application to Mr. ROBERT TURNBULL, Superintendent of the Line, Euston Station, London, N.W., or to Mr. G. CALTHROP, General Superintendent, Caledonian Railway, 302 Buchanan Street, Glasgow.

The Minimum Charges for Saloon and Family Carriages are as follow :—
For a Family Carriage—Four First Class and Four Third Class Fares.
For a Saloon—First Class Tickets must be taken equivalent in value to Four First Class and Four Third Class Fares.
Each Passenger travelling must hold a ticket corresponding with the class of carriage used, and if the party in any case exceeds the number named above, an additional Fare must be paid for each additional Passenger.

Engaged Compartments.

Compartments can be engaged on application to the Station Masters at the principal Stations on the London and North-Western and Caledonian Railways for not less than Four First or Four Third Class Passengers holding tickets between England and Scotland. If more than four seats are occupied in a Reserved Compartment the additional Fares must be paid.

Through Guards.

Guards taking charge of the Through Luggage travel by the Express Trains between London (Euston), Liverpool (Lime Street or Exchange), Manchester (Exchange or Victoria), Glasgow (Central), Edinburgh (Princes Street), and Perth, Dundee (West), and Aberdeen.

HOTEL ACCOMMODATION
ON WEST COAST ROUTE.

Passengers wishing to stay at the Hotels under the management of the West Coast Companies may, on stating their requirements to the Station Master at any of these Companies' Stations, have a telegram sent free ordering the necessary accommodation. The following are the Hotels to which this arrangement will apply :—

LONDON (EUSTON HOTEL).
BLETCHLEY.
BIRMINGHAM (QUEEN'S HOTEL).
CREWE (CREWE ARMS).
HOLYHEAD (STATION HOTEL).
DUBLIN (NORTH WESTERN HOTEL).
GREENORE.
LIVERPOOL (NORTH WESTERN HOTEL).
PRESTON (PARK HOTEL).
GLASGOW (CENTRAL STATION HOTEL).
EDINBURGH (PRINCES STREET STATION HOTEL).
PERTH (GENERAL STATION HOTEL).

The accommodation provided at these Hotels is of the highest standard, and the charges will be found to be reasonable.

1581, 0-4-2 built 1871.

LOCKERBIE STATION.